Ten Things

Your Student with Autism Wishes You Knew

Ellen Notbohm

with Veronica Zysk

Ten Things

Your Student With Autism Wishes You Knew

All marketing and publishing rights guaranteed to and reserved by

FUTURE HORIZONS INC.

721 W. Abram Street
Arlington, TX 76013

800-489-0727

817-277-0727

817-277-2270 Fax

Website: www.FHautism.com
E-mail: info@FHautism.com

Cover design and text layout by Matt Mitchell, mattmitchelldesign.com

ISBN: 1-932565-36-1

ISBN-13: 978-1-932565-36-2

What readers say about

Ten Things Your Student With Autism Wishes You Knew
Winner of a 2006 iParenting Media Award

"Valuable guidance for educators who wish to understand the thinking patterns of students with autism in order to teach them most effectively."

Elizabeth Mumper, MD
CEO, Advocates for Children
Medical Director, Defeat Autism Now! Physician Training
Co-Chair, Autism Research Institute Advisory Board

"Ellen's amazing ability to reach deep inside the minds of these very special children is a gift that keeps on giving. For everyone involved in their lives, Ellen's clarity and straightforwardness is 'must' reading!"

Charles D. Hammerman, Managing Director, The Burton Blatt Institute, Syracuse University

"Ellen provides an excellent introductory perspective for those involved with educating children on the autism spectrum. Her work is practical, concise and brimming with common sense. I particularly applaud her emphasis on raising our expectations for autistic learners and getting to know children with autism as people, rather than diagnoses or problems."

Steven E. Gutstein, PhD
Founder, Relationship Development Intervention (RDI)
Director, The Connections Center, Houston, Texas

"I hope every teacher, family member, and friend reads Ellen's new book Ten Things Your Student With Autism Wishes You Knew. *There is something very special in it for all of us."*

Candace K. Ganz, Ed.D., CCC-SLP
Project Director, Nevada Autism Summit
Assistant Director, Nevada UCED
University of Nevada, Reno

"Ellen captures the major issues of autism and makes them understandable and useable, even to those new to spectrum disorders. The simplicity and depth of explanations gives me hope that all kids on the spectrum will soon be understood and accepted for what they CAN do and not defined by their limitations. I am thrilled with Ellen's concise and yet compassionate approach. Here at Unlocking Autism (a National Autism Awareness Organization) and the UA Call Center and Hotline, I am anxious to share with the thousands of callers I speak with each year this valuable information."

Nancy H. Cale, Vice President, Unlocking Autism

Also by Ellen Notbohm:

Ten Things Every Child with Autism Wishes You Knew

ForeWord 2005 Book of the Year Award,
Honorable Mention
Winner of a 2005 iParenting Media Award

1001 Great Ideas for Teaching and Raising Children with Autism Spectrum Disorders

(with Veronica Zysk)

Learning Magazine's
Teachers' Choice Award for 2006

For Connor and Bryce
...as if my books could be anything but

Acknowledgments

My work on this book coincided with my son Connor's last semester of high school, so it was only natural that I spent some time reflecting on the constellation of educators with whom we've interacted on behalf of both of our sons over the past sixteen years. I started a list but lost count after 100. Of that 100, there were three genuine stinkers, and perhaps a handful were questionable. The rest of them, the bountiful majority, ranged from very good to simply superlative. They ply their excellent work under increasingly difficult conditions, and the dedication they display is humbling. I could never do what they do, and I salute every one of them.

The hearts and minds of so many of those teachers and therapists are embodied in this book. Some I have named in specific passages and some I have not, either because they asked not to be identified, or because their ideas are presented as composite with other similar-thinkers. Either way, please join me in hoping that all kids with autism get to have educators and service providers like those whose ideas shine throughout this book: Roneete Lynas, Ariel Nadel, Christine Hunt, Jackie Druck, Mary Schunk, Nola Shirley, Veda Nomura, Julieann Barker, Christine Bemrose, Sarah Spella, Patti Rawding-Anderson, to name only a few.

Special thanks to Jennifer McIlwee Myers, self-described Aspie at Large, for clear-eyed and compelling insights into what it's like to navigate life and the education system as a child with AS.

Thanks as always to Wayne Gilpin and the staff of Future Horizons, with extra credit going to my editorial coordinator Kelly Gilpin, who makes the job of babysitting me look easy.

And to my personal support staff: my steadfast husband Mark, my matchless mother Henny Bernstein, my son Connor, my late father David (who still manages to convey his pride from wherever he is in the cosmos), my Uncle Leonard and Aunt Barbara Bock, and wonder-friend Lori Heimbichner. Pom-pom in one hand, pen in the other, her encouragement and astute comments on the manuscript contributed to a richer finished product.

As for my editor Veronica Zysk, she supersedes words. The original concept and vision for this book were hers, and I thank her for not accepting less than she knew me to be capable of, particularly when "forceps delivery" of certain chapters became necessary. She is the co-author of Chapter Three because the breadth and depth of her understanding of the subject demanded a voice in this book.

But in the end, as always, there would be no book without Bryce. Wherever he is headed is where I'm going. *I wonder where ...*

Contents

Preface

In the spring of 2004, I wrote a short piece called *Ten Things Every Child with Autism Wishes You Knew*. I did it on a semi-dare: I had seen a wish-list type article written by a mother to a teacher, and I had seen articles written from a teacher's point of view, but I had never seen anything written from the child's point of view. I should do this, I remarked offhandedly to my editor, Veronica Zysk. Yes, you should, came the reply.

The piece flowed out of me freely, as if coming from some natural part of the landscape. What I could not have imagined was the response. It traveled the Internet like wildfire and hit print in dozens of publications on every continent (okay, not Antarctica). Within the year, a book based on the article followed, and it too brought new friends to me from around the world.

When I started getting requests for more articles of a similar nature, I had to ponder what about this original piece resonated so deeply among such a diverse group of people. Readers made it clear that it was the fact it spoke with a child's voice, a voice not heard often enough. It's not surprising that this voice is not heard when one of the hallmarks of autism is its veritable steeplechase of obstacles to effective communication.

There was and is great need—and more and more I'm sensing, great willingness—to understand the world as children with autism experience it. So the voice of our child returned in a second article, *Ten Things Your Student with Autism Wishes You Knew*, to tell us what children with autism wish their teachers knew. It too became a torch passed from reader to reader around the world. It was only a matter of time until my publisher and editor suggested—firmly—that this book was the next step both natural and necessary. At the same time I was hearing from teachers, preschool through university, who wanted to use my articles as handouts and training materials for family members, caregivers, administrators and staff. The child's voice provided a compelling starting point for easing the general population into the shift in thinking so necessary if we are to succeed in reaching and teaching our children with autism.

There are two over-arching reasons I am able to write this book. The first is that, from the moment I heard the word "autism" applied to my son, Bryce, I was determined to play the hand we'd been dealt without bitterness and without blame, in as constructive and positive and healthy a manner as we could possibly achieve. The second reason is that, although I had already (obviously) signed on for my role as a parent, I realized quickly that I would have to step up to the fact that I would be wearing a teacher's hat for far more than table manners and tying shoelaces. I would have to teach things I didn't know yet and I would have to teach them in a manner that was not the slightest bit familiar to me. In other words, I would have to be learner first, before I could be a teacher.

This is the dangerous juncture at which, whether "teacher" means educator or parent, it is easy to become overwhelmed. There is so much about autism we don't know or understand! There is so much this child needs to learn! There are only six hours in the school day! There are only 175 days in a school year! There are only fifteen (or less!) years left until he is an adult! Yes, I needed to become a learner first, but the first thing I needed to learn was how to "pace the race." I didn't need to know everything up front; I could and would learn as we went along. I only needed to know enough to stay one step ahead of my son, still within beckoning distance, just enough to be able to kick the can the next little piece farther down the road. Equally important was learning that I couldn't go this alone—and that I wouldn't have to. Although Bryce would be my primary teacher, all sorts of others—children and adults— would have a hand in teaching me as well.

What is it about any teacher that incites learning, makes us curious about our world? Aren't we all more open to learning when we feel we can truly trust the messenger, feel that both our efforts and our personal way of thinking and doing are respected? If we feel validated by our teachers as individual selves, we are more willing to take the risks necessary to learning. Don't we all respond more eagerly to those who actively believe in us—as opposed to those who communicate indifference, doubt or resignation?

I won't say this was easy, but it works. And it worked for my son because he—my whole family—had the immeasurable advantage of learning from immensely talented and caring teachers every step of the way. But hear this clearly: we weren't "lucky." I looked at dozens of schools within the 25-mile radius surrounding our home until I found the one that stood out as being the right fit for our sons. We took fairly drastic steps to get our sons into that school. What those steps were is not as important as the fact that we were willing to do whatever it took, because the very culture of the teaching community at that school was what our sons needed in order to succeed. What I learned alongside the many dedicated teachers who've worked with

Bryce was the impetus for this book. Their voices ring throughout, whether identified or not.

My search for the right school had pretty much narrowed down to The One as I interviewed the last of the neighborhood parents and professionals on my list. Eerily, I began to hear the same remark over and over: "Oh yes, it's a wonderful school. But whatever you do, when you get to third grade, make sure you get Jackie, the teacher to end all teachers!" I found out that Jackie Druck had this "rep" going back literally decades. When we did "get" Jackie for third grade, I spent about as much time in the classroom as Bryce would allow. And I became enormously baffled. For such a grandiose reputation, Jackie was a very low-key, unassuming person; her classroom was calm and orderly, the peaceful, fluid music of Enya often playing softly. I could not for the life of me put my finger on any specific thing she was doing that kept two generations of kids, including Bryce, so spellbound.

And yet.

When the kids all wrote their year-end essays highlighting their favorite parts of third grade, it was clear that most, if not all, were simply in love with her. When she retired shortly thereafter, the party for her had to be held in a city park in order to accommodate all who wanted to come.

I had to mull over all this with my old college girlfriend Shirley, herself a nationally board-certified teacher. Shirley and Jackie have never met and yet Shirley didn't hesitate to answer my question. "I can tell you what it is," she said. "I'd be willing to bet she has a deep, deep inherent respect for each child and that she communicates that to them.

Children are willing to do quite a bit for teachers who first and foremost respect them as individuals."

Two very telling exchanges unfolded at the beginning of our year in Jackie's classroom. At our first meeting, she told me she was very excited about the opportunity to work with Bryce. She had, she said, taught only one other student with autism, a few years earlier, and he had been quite different from Bryce. I had to smile just a little, as I gently told her: if you have been teaching for 35 years, you have had far more than one. You just didn't know what you were looking at. Sure enough, a few weeks later I got a call. You are right, she said. I have had dozens of them. *How much more I could have done if I had known.*

Jackie's willingness to be a lifelong learner, her curiosity, her respect for all manner of learners was indeed the "secret" of her success. At parent conferences two months into the school year, she greeted me with, "I'm going to have to keep him for a couple of years."

I was stunned. I had thought things were going so well. "Is he doing that poorly?" I asked.

"No, silly," she said. "I am just that intrigued by him.

"There is so much more I need to learn about him. From him."

We begin again ...

Some of you will have read the original article *Ten Things Your Student with Autism Wishes You Knew*, and you will undoubtedly note that the Ten Things in this book are not the same Ten Things enumerated in the article. And yet they are. Everything that was in the article is included as part of this book. But it has become much more in that I have "gone global," gone beyond specific suggestions for the classroom and folded those ideas into the larger concepts that should govern the teacher in all of us, whether trained educator, support staff, parent, therapist, administrator, family member—or Quidditch coach! Actually, for those of you familiar with the Harry Potter saga, did you ever notice that the Quidditch teams have no coaches? They are completely student-led units, left to win or lose on their own experiences and devices with no adult guidance. And *that's* why they call it magic!

So this book does contain strategies and tactics, but not as the primary focus. Strategies and tactics are vital and necessary; they are the nuts and bolts of the educational quest. But we want to go beyond that, to consider how smoothly the whole locomotive will chug after all the bolts are in place, after adding the fuel that will enable it to move. A former in-law of mine headed up the aircraft maintenance operation at an Air Force base. He summed up this very critical job as "tightening up the loose stuff and loosening up the tight stuff." And so it is with fine-tuning a whole child. Their future success is predicated on much more than the facts we teach them.

To be able to hear the voice of our student with autism and respond in ways that are meaningful to him or her, we must be able to step outside our own deeply ingrained frame of reference. Most of us think in words, this child may think in pictures. We embrace the nuances of language, he needs concrete explanations. We infer context and motivation from our observations of others, he is "mindblind" to such social subtleties. What smells good to us makes him nauseous, and sounds that we routinely "filter out" make his head pound.

Nearly every teacher with whom I've spent any time at all tells me that the real magic lies in "seeing the light bulb go on," with any child. If you can't find the switch, the groping can get frustrating. My hope is that this book will guide your hand, with the magic of simplicity and common sense, to that switch. It is at the same time easier than you think and more challenging than you think.

Much of this book will involve exploring the ways in which your students with autism experience the typical landscape differently—the different manner in which they think, relate socially to others, process sensory input. But as teachers and parent-teachers, we must never lose sight of the fact that ASD (autism spectrum disorder) children also share many characteristics with typical children. The Ten Things we lay out in this book are critical to teaching ASD children. But you will find much that benefits typical children as well.

In the end, it's not about "singling out" the ASD child for "special treatment." It's about teaching to the strengths and deficits of a different kind of learner. Progress will come; progress *will* come. You'll see the light bulb click on (albeit in perhaps unpredictable increments), and the results will be exciting. Isn't that why you became a teacher in the first place? Let's get started.

Here are ten things your student
with autism wishes you knew.

LEARNING IS CIRCULAR
We are all both teachers and students.

Remember the old "I'm a Pepper" Dr. Pepper commercial? I changed it a little bit for us:

> I'm a teacher, you're a teacher,
> he's a teacher, we're all teachers,
> wouldn't you like to be a teacher too?

Learning flows in all directions, not only from you as the teacher to me as the student, but from student to teacher, from student to student, and from teacher to teacher. This circle of learning is what makes it work for all of us. Think of what happens when teaching isn't circular, when teachers can only think on a one-way street. There is that scene in a very funny movie called *Ferris Bueller's Day Off*. A kid is asleep with his head on the desk in a puddle of drool while the teacher talks on and on. I'm pretty sure that student's not learning anything.

The world is like a double-sided 2000-piece jigsaw puzzle of learning opportunities. But my autism can make it difficult for me to recognize those opportunities. I don't learn in ways most people do; my autism way of thinking interferes with my ability to understand the information that surrounds me. But here's one thing about learning that I do know: you have as much to learn from me as I do from you.

Students with autism need teachers who love being learners, too. You will help me learn things I need to know, and what you learn from me is very important, too—because there are more like me headed your way.

WE ARE A TEAM
Success depends on all of us working together.

I usually think of "team" as being a sports word. The players play different positions but they wear the same clothes so everyone can easily see that they are all working together to accomplish something. Each player is important and the team members depend on each other. They share their wins and their losses together, slap high-fives when one of them does something great. They help each other out when one of them is having a bad day.

I looked up "team" in the dictionary and I think we should all paste this definition on our bathroom mirrors: "team: a group of people who share a purpose or task and depend on each other over an extended period of time to succeed." I may or may not be very good at sports, but as a child with autism, having people around me who want to play on MY team is the very thing I need to succeed, and nothing less.

I THINK DIFFERENTLY
Teach me in a way that is meaningful to me.

Because I think differently, my autism requires that you teach differently. In order to teach me to color inside the lines, you may have to reach outside those lines. To get me to see life and learning as a palette of colors, you have to start by understanding that through my eyes, life's experiences are black and white, all or nothing.

Autism is a different way of *thinking*. My brain works differently than yours. Yet your way of thinking is so natural to you that you cannot even imagine that *it is foreign to me.*

For you, the relationships among the things you learn, the things that happen to you and the people around you form naturally and without structured teaching. For me, all of these parts exist in independent, unrelated cells, and I can't connect the dots. Each dot stands alone.

Please realize how deeply this different way of thinking affects learning, and teach me in a manner that respects who I am—a child with autism.

BEHAVIOR IS COMMUNICATION: YOURS, MINE AND OURS

All behavior occurs for a reason. Behavior is information about what is happening between you and me, and about how factors we can or can't see in our environment affect me. It tells you, even when my words can't, how I perceive what is happening around me. When you try to change my behavior without finding its source, everyone's behaviors will change—for the worse!

Start by believing this: I truly do want to learn to interact appropriately. Negative behavior interferes with my learning process, and no child wants or likes getting his or her feelings crushed by the reactions we get to our "bad" behavior. Such behavior usually means one or more of my senses has gone into overload, or I cannot communicate my wants or needs, or I don't understand what is expected of me.

Behavior is a symptom. Look beyond the behavior to find the source of my discomfort. Merely getting me to stop these behaviors is not enough; it doesn't address the basic cause or need. Identify that—then teach me to exchange these behaviors with acceptable (to both of us) choices so that real learning can flow.

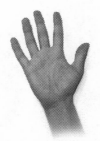

GLITCHED, GARBLED AND BEWILDERED

If we can't communicate effectively,
learning can't happen.

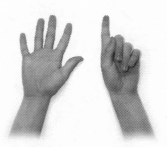

TEACH THE WHOLE ME
I'm much more than a set of "broken" or "missing" parts.

I'm a kid. When I look in the mirror, that's what I see—a kid, not "issues" or "symptoms" or "deficits." Like you, I am a one-of-a-kind combination of body, mind and spirit. Like you, I have a unique personality with my own thoughts and ideas, quirks, preferences, dreams and fears.

Learning should be a whole-person thing. Teach *me*, the whole child, not a collection of symptoms or missing skills, or a set of pieces. Merely teaching me facts or skills with no social or emotional connectivity between them may not be teaching me much at all.

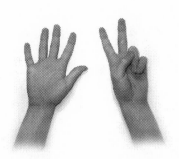

BE CURIOUS
...be very curious.

When I was learning to read, my speech teacher would "picture walk" through books with me. On each page, we would look at the picture and say, "I wonder." *I wonder what will happen next? I wonder why she looks sad? I wonder who is at the door?* Together we would find the answers to all of our "I wonder" questions.

Be curious about what makes me tick, and about the road less traveled you may have to tread in order to reach me. Like many children with autism, I am not a Curious George or Georgette, so I need you to be doubly so. Your curiosity will show me wonderful, wonderful things: first and foremost, that you care about me. Second, that beyond rote repetition, beyond what I need to do merely to get by, real learning will happen, only when I finally feel able to move out of my slender comfort zone and into a world that is frequently fearful and overwhelming to me. And most importantly, I will learn that genuinely interesting and enjoyable experiences await me if I can allow myself to be curious.

I wonder: how much can we learn together if we can remember to be curious?

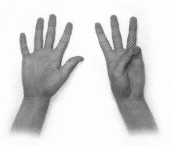

CAN I TRUST YOU?

Build my trust in you, because if and only if I can trust you will learning unfold freely. Just because you are an authority figure doesn't mean I will automatically trust you. I may comply with your instructions but that is not the same as trust. I will trust someone who respects my individual needs and does his or her best to meet them, and I will trust someone who is honest with me, even when—especially when—they don't know all the answers.

When I can trust you, I can more easily see that what you are trying to teach me is truly relevant to me (it is, isn't it?). When I can trust you, I can learn to trust myself. And when I can trust myself, just watch me learn!

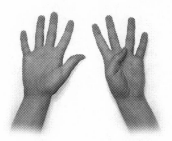

BELIEVE

That car guy Henry Ford said, "Whether you think you can or whether you think you can't, you are usually right."

Believe that I can learn and I will learn.

Believe that you can make a difference for me and you will.

Encourage me to be everything I can be, so I can stay the course long after I've left your classroom.

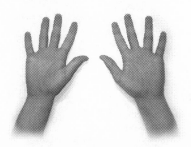

TEACH ME "HOW TO FISH"
See me as a capable adult and hold that vision.

The Chinese have a saying: "Give a man a fish and you feed him for a day. Teach a man to fish and you feed him for a lifetime." The most important things you can teach me will not necessarily be found in a book or on a worksheet. I need to learn skills to live my adult life as independently and productively as possible.

Make learning relevant for me. Teach me how to use knowledge in a functional way to life as an independent and *interdependent* adult—able to take care of myself, but also able to interact effectively with coworkers, neighbors, friends and people of the world in general.

Fishing is the art of casting out my line and the science of reeling in my "catch." Teach me both the art and science of my life.

Chapter One

LEARNING IS CIRCULAR
We are all both teachers and students.

The notion that learning is circular is neither new nor unique. Many of Bryce's teachers have told me they learned a great deal from him, and that they learn continually from all the children they teach. This seems not only natural to me, but exhilarating.

Yet I still remember hearing one mom who bridled at these kinds of remarks. "I'm so tired of hearing teachers say they've learned so much from my kid! I want them to teach him, not learn from him." Reading between her lines, I heard an anxious urgency, the vastness of all she felt her son needed to learn colliding with the real-world limitations of a six-hour school day. We have all been frequent visitors to that impatient place, but we need to remind ourselves that it's counterproductive. Teachers themselves must take advantage of the learning opportunities as they present; passing up those opportunities in the name of saving time will eventually only slow the teaching process. How could it be otherwise?

Because I have learned side by side with so many outstanding teachers over the years, I've lived the power of circular learning in action, where teaching and learning energies zoom the circuits back and forth between all individuals, of all ages and all stations in education and in life. It started right at the beginning, when Bryce was in preschool. The very gifted "Teacher Christine" Hunt truly walked the talk of circular learning. Before our year together was out, she was insisting that I must write a book. Then she romped on me for seven years until I actually did it.

No less a teacher was Veda Nomura, the occupational therapist who was part of Bryce's team of teachers. Veda patiently, patiently guided not just Bryce but me as well to understanding the devilishly complicated landscape of sensory integration. It was one of the toughest propositions I ever confronted in my life. When I finally succeeded, I had Veda on a pedestal so high as to induce vertigo.

Across a wall in Teacher Christine's classroom was a display. The children each contributed a photo of themselves along with a paper that filled in the phrase "I am learning to _____." Bryce wrote that he was learning to ride a training-wheel bike. But I was particularly smitten with what Veda wrote: "I am learning to raise teenagers," it said. Her statement really brought home to me that no matter how knowledgeable and capable any one of us may seem, we are all still learning, still searching for the best way to handle new challenges.

Just about any book you pick up calls autism a "mystery," but I don't like that word. I'm not interested in whodunit. I want to know what comes next. And because I want to know what comes next, I don't like the implication of the word "mystery" if it suggests that "unknown" is synonymous with "unknowable." Just as a good mystery dissolves in the hands of a good detective, autism is knowable. It's just that children with autism are not prepackaged fare: no two are exactly alike, no one intervention is a sure thing and achieving success with a child is too often a matter of discovering what doesn't work, as much as discovering what does. It can be exhausting and exasperating, but never does it constitute failure. "Results!" Thomas Edison once said. "Why, man, I have gotten a lot of results. I know several thousand things that won't work."

German philosopher Martin Heidegger tells us, "Teaching is more difficult than learning because what teaching calls for is this: to let learn." That is an explosive, double-barreled concept, but the absolute embodiment of circular learning. As adults, we bear the burden; we must relinquish all our conceits and presumptions in order to let ourselves learn what we need to know to be able to teach a child with autism, whose thoughts originate in a frame of reference completely different from our own. Venturing into a place where we don't know the lay of the land and don't have all the answers can be intimidating, no question. *"If, as a teacher, you find that an uncomfortable place to be, I understand,"* says your student with autism. *"That's how I feel quite a lot of the time, when so very often I don't know the answers."* This holds true for professionals and parents. But it's not a reason to "not go there." A friend of ours once left a comfortable teaching job at a so-called nice school to take a job across town as assistant principal at a so-called tough school. We simply couldn't believe it, but when we asked him why, he said that he considered it "an acceptable challenge." Discomfort is a good thing when we can use it as impetus to squirm to the next level.

And then, when we have let ourselves learn well, we need to let our student learn. By its very nature, this cannot be a pain-free process, for us or for the child. The best among us will question whether we got it right, whether or what we could have done better. Did we hurt the child, who already struggles so because of his autism, unintentionally and/or needlessly?

I can still scarcely bear to think about all the mistakes I made with my son when I was in the early stages of learning—from him, not from books—about his autism. But for all the times I beat myself up black and blue, there was a teacher on the other end of the phone saying: This happens to all of us, Ellen. As parents and as teachers. He will forgive you if you forgive yourself.

He and I both learned to push the boundaries of our resilience, and we learned from each other. Freely admitting my mistakes to him was a very powerful learning tool. No one is infallible, and increasingly it struck me as odd that we set up children to "respect authority" without ever considering that they might respect us more if we were honest about our humanity. As a parent and as his first-and-always teacher, I never hesitate to apologize to Bryce (or Connor, my older son) when I am wrong. Whether it's because I misjudged, was careless, didn't have the right information or simply should have known better, it's more meaningful for him in the long run to pull him into the circle of life-learning where we can approach mistakes with curiosity rather than self-flagellation and say, "Whoa! That didn't work. I wonder what we could try next?" or "We'll do better next time."

Our student with autism relies on us, as the adults in his life, to learn about him from each other, too. Reading through my mailbag can be poignant. Parents tell me how much they have to share with their child's educators about his autism, if only they would listen and respect a parent's wisdom born of experience. Educators lament parents who resist, reject, disbelieve and deny their professional observations and suggestions, even those based on what they learn from experience with the child during the school day.

Circular learning challenges us to lay aside our egos and become child-centered in our approach, to embrace the process as well as outcome, and to "boldly go" off the beaten path, outside the lane lines, to willingly bump down the road less traveled. It challenges us to place less value on test scores and the top-down approach, and rather turn our efforts towards relationship-building, cooperation and reigniting the thrill of exploration. Circular learning acknowledges that true teaching isn't only about putting information into the minds of our students, rather it is *striving to bring something out of every learner.* That "learner" is not just the student with autism; it's you, and me and everyone with whom he will interact.

Accepting the notion that I must be a full partner and fellow learner in Bryce's education was something I accepted from Day One. I always knew intuitively that my mission was to prepare Bryce to live as a capable, independent adult. And yet when our child is so very young and the obstacles thrown up by autism seem so very threatening, it is only natural that we cling to "lifeboats" who come along in the form of wise and effective teachers. One such person for me was Nola Shirley, one of Bryce's first paraeducators. More than one teacher referred to her as a miracle worker, and we will hear more about her secret of success later in the book. But for now, we step into her circle of learning at the "parent as learner" stop.

Far from limiting herself to teaching only Bryce, she played a major role in teaching me, as a parent, about independence too. She had seen Bryce through two years of kindergarten and on through first grade before judging, reluctantly, that he was becoming too dependent upon her and it was time to step away. In hindsight I am forced to wonder if it was really Bryce who was becoming too dependent upon her—or me. I can still feel the sickening lurch my stomach took when, at the end of that first grade year, I opened her note that read: "What a wonderful year we have had. I will not be working with Bryce in second grade. I hope that the friendships we have forged in the last few years can last a lifetime." Later she told me she knew it was time to step away when she realized that he would look to her automatically, even for tasks of which he was well capable.

In this regard, it's clear that Bryce was more teachable than I was. He moved on to become ever more independent while I, ten years after our first hello, still scurry back to Nola for answers, especially when I already know the answer but don't like it. She's my paraeducator too, but in my case, it's a lifetime assignment. Our circle will be unbroken. This year she sat next to me at a very special birthday party—mine, hosted by Teacher Christine, Teacher Veda and other friends from that first preschool team. None of us can imagine going through the last decade without the exchange of insights, experiences and support that has traveled our "continuous loop."

Disney's 1995 movie *Pocahontas* eloquently made the case for circular learning in the popular song, "The Colors of the Wind." Pocahontas tells John Smith, "We are all connected to each other in a circle...that never ends." She admonishes him for being unable to value people who don't "think like you":

> ...But if you walk the footsteps of a stranger,
> *You'll learn things you never knew you never knew.*

If as teachers we are ever to feel comfortable and confident with autism, recognizing the teacher that lies within each of our students with autism is the foundation of any success we will achieve. It speaks to trust, respect, and the value of every individual, building blocks without which real learning cannot flourish. The first Yellow Brick in the road is that wonderfully empowering acceptance that every moment is a teaching and learning moment, and that we are all both teachers and students. If autism is a mystery, the next question should be howdunit?, not whodunit? It's an invitation to a dynamic partnership, to create multi-dimensional spheres of learning for all of us—but especially for the student with autism.

Step right up. He's counting on you.

Chapter Two

WE ARE A TEAM
Success depends on all of us
working together.

Just as it takes a village to raise a child, it takes a team to educate a child with autism. And just as nature does, education should abhor a vacuum. Teachers don't teach in a vacuum, parents don't rear their children in a vacuum, children don't develop in any significant way in a vacuum. That goes double for the child with autism, whose many social, sensory and communication challenges may make that vacuum look like a mighty comfortable place. Good team dynamics are a must if we are in fact to succeed with our student over an extended period of time.

At the beginning of our odyssey, I had the painful but timely experience of seeing poor teamwork in action. Bryce had been placed in an early intervention preschool classroom conveniently housed at our neighborhood school. Children with various social communication difficulties (autism, Asperger's syndrome, ADHD, brain injury) made up half the class; "neighborhood peers" completed the group. Basing this region-wide class in our neighborhood school was fortuitous—it would give us a glimpse into what the school would be like for Bryce when he reached kindergarten age the following year.

I was intellectually out the door of that school the very minute I heard that a primary grade teacher had asked one of my son's paraeducators, with dripping sarcasm, "And what exactly is it that you expect to accomplish with these kids?" Even if that particular teacher was the only one in the building giving off those kinds of noxious fumes—and I considered it unlikely, given trickle-down thinking—it still meant that everyone around her was breathing them. I looked around the rest of the school. I saw a tired principal who was only a year or two away from retirement. I saw a teaching staff with low morale, first grades with 32 kids, endemic behavior problems that were not being addressed. My search for a healthier environment was on.

We ended up at Capitol Hill, a school whose culture reflected, blindingly, the worth and importance of all learners. The principal filled empty classrooms with special-needs preschool programs. The school didn't have a soccer team or an orchestra, but instead used discretionary funds for a full-time child development specialist, who was available for everything from individual counseling to small group discussions to whole-class lessons on social dynamics. The resource/learning center was located in the hub of the school, not some dark, out-of-the-way corner, and so many kids landed there for help that no stigma was ever attached. The school loudly trumpeted its status as a "No Put-down Zone," and incidences of unkindness in any form were dealt with speedily and firmly. The school reverberated with the spirit of teamwork.

Bryce attended Capitol Hill for seven years. He received services that increased where needed with each passing year. His teachers loved him to bits and the principal defended him fiercely when necessary. He progressed gracefully, each year beginning with virtually no regression and with enthusiasm bred of the comfort of familiarity. With the skill of an Olympic relay team, he was handed off from each grade to the next by teachers who understood the importance of sharing their insights. All the mutual enthusiasm was infectious and produced big results.

As adults, we have to be very careful of straying too far from that bathroom-mirror definition of "team" as a group of people whose success at their shared task demands interdependence of effort. We allow ourselves to get too far beyond planning sound moves and strategies, into the politics, the finger-pointing, the fake-'em-outs, the he-said-she-said. These are not good team dynamics. Your student with autism needs an effective multi-disciplinary team. What does an effective team look like? Mommy or Daddy yelling at teachers? Teachers not returning Mom's calls? The immovable preconceived assumption meeting the irresistible unsubstantiated stereotype? Dueling lawyers? Tolerating teasing and taunting because "that's what kids do?"

For the record, I truly believe this behavior is not yours. But it's out there. Every year teachers face new parents and parents face new teachers. And isn't that great? Talk about "equal opportunity"! It's all good, if we allow it to be.

In our ever-evolving circle of learning, the components of team dynamics are simple:

- The actions we display to each other

- The attitudes we display to each other.

These components come in three flavors: productive, indifferent or poisonous. We are the ones with the power to make the choice among those three. For our student with autism and his teachers, be they parent or educators, choosing to be a productive team player is a make-or-break-this-child choice.

What makes for productive team dynamics? Good team dynamics are a set of ground rules that all parties ascribe to because they know that the whole is more than merely the sum of all parts. Were this not true, we could make a human being by swishing 35 liters of water, 20 kilograms of carbon and four liters of ammonia with the proper quantities of lime, phosphorus, salt, sulfur, iron, silicon and a bunch of other trace elements. But of course that wouldn't create a person, it would only create a swamp—because the sum of the parts does not achieve the whole. It takes a little biochemical magic as well.

We need biochemical magic in our relationships as educational team members. In this real-life lab, the nucleus is the teacher and the child, and it grows from there. Designate a "proton" right from the start, a team leader with a positive charge who will set the tone, establish and maintain the underlying current that will guide the team interactions. Then set up the formula.

PRODUCTIVE TEAM DYNAMICS

Assembling the team. Defining who is on the team, or who needs to be added to or dropped from the team has to be the first step. In many cases, team members may be dictated by the IEP. But even if that isn't the case, it's hard for me to imagine a young child with autism whose team would consist of anything less than the parent(s), the classroom teacher, the special educator, an occupational therapist and a speech/language therapist. It can certainly grow from there, and the composition of the team will change and evolve as the child does.

Communication, communication, communication. Just as location is everything in real estate, communication is everything in teamwork.

- Between home and school. Accept no substitutes!

    - Daily: It's not possible to overstate the value of communication going back and forth between home and school, on a daily basis if possible. It's a long time between 3:00 pm and 8:00 am—let alone weekends—and much can happen in those hours that will impact the student's school day. It's a long time between 8:00 am and 3:00 pm for Mom, too. What does her child do all day? When he comes home he is exhausted and doesn't want to or isn't able to talk, to converse. Regular communication between home and school enhances team members' ability to support each others' efforts and adds a consistency to the child's routine that smoothes the daily transitions. It serves to head off some problems, nip others in the bud, celebrate achievements in both settings. It communicates to the child that we are all on the same side.

    Daily communication needn't be prohibitively time-consuming. It can be as simple as a couple of lines scribbled in a spiral notebook that goes back and forth in the student's backpack each day, or just bullet-pointed emails. The important thing is to recognize it as the ounce of effort that saves pounds of guessing, defensive reacting or simply not knowing.

- Big picture: Parents, a teacher pal of mine asked me to be sure to tell you: "Don't assume I know everything about your child. I may only have the prior year's academic information and perhaps no personal information at all. Be a resource for us, a bridge between programs."

Teachers, you know that many typically developing kids give their parents little information about their school day. For your student with autism, this is magnified by his difficulty with verbalization, sequencing, generalization and retrieval, not to mention the exhaustion he feels after an entire day's effort of having to "hold it together." Don't make his parents beg you for information. In addition to daily home-school communication, respect that quarterly IEP progress reports are mandatory and must happen in timely fashion.

- Between members of the team within a school. Productive team members recognize that shared information and exchange of ideas is what makes the typical "division of labor" work. It also communicates on a wider platform those same shared discoveries and concerns between home and school.

Recognizing the entire class as a team or community, working as a whole, toward inclusion. "This is how society works successfully," asserts fourth grade teacher Roneete Lynas, who describes herself as "a huge advocate and proponent of the 'classroom community.' There should be no reason why students and teachers alike are not sharing the responsibility of including *all* learners." Knowing how to

14

work as a member of a community is as crucial a life skill as anything coming out of a book.

Promoting a cycle of encouragement and reward—not only teacher to student, but student to student and teacher to teacher. Instill the idea of taking responsibility for one's self as the first step, not the end goal. "Life rewards us for acting responsibly," Roneete adds, "but we benefit more fully and more wholly when acting cooperatively." The class team who together reaps either reward or consequence learns a lesson that they will carry into the workplace, interpersonal relationships and civic life in general as adults, that they have the power to create the most successful environment if working as a team.

Giving each other the courtesy of a clean slate. Parents may have had bad experiences with previous teachers or schools, but putting past conflicts or issues onto a new teacher, "coming in with guns blazing before you even have a chance to get to know me or my program," as one put it, is counterproductive. *This is what has happened in the past and I expect the same from you* sets up a scenario that is dangerous for teacher as well as parent. Teachers, your previous experiences with ASD students and/or their parents, whether frustrating or even successful, may have little relevance to this student. Is there any bigger waste of time than anticipating trouble, possibly where none exists?

An understanding that the team is not static. The team will evolve as the child grows and changes, and that's okay. Listen as objectively as possible when one team member says something isn't working. When transition to a different setting seems necessary, let it happen in the spirit of wanting a common good for the child. Evaluate as neutrally as possible: if the child is struggling too hard in the current placement, it's time to find a better environment.

Eyes on the prize. The team recognizes that the job of parents and educators is to prepare this young person for real life wherein his success is going to depend upon much more than test scores and transcripts. Even in the face of today's crushing test requirements, Roneete Lynas prompts us to "sit back and remind ourselves that students are not under our instruction to become little 'experts,' merely regurgitating information. Rather, they are placed in our hands to be *guided* throughout the year. They are truly *practicing for real life*, for the entire course of this school year—until the next comes, with its new expectations."

INDIFFERENT TEAM DYNAMICS

An attitude that the special needs student is someone else's responsibility. It's the classroom teacher who says: I have thirty other students; he's the responsibility of the resource teacher (or the paraeducator). It's the parent who says: I feed and clothe him. You're the school—so teach him.

Good teams can fall apart quickly when members rely, either consciously or out of benign neglect, on someone else to do the heavy lifting. An effective team stays strong when all members contribute relevant and timely information regarding both the individual child and the state of current knowledge, research and attitudes about the disability itself. This sharing of responsibility and insight is the only sensible way for everyone to keep up in any meaningful way in a field like autism, where both information and identified incidences are on a swift and steep ascent.

Accepting "good enough" as good enough. It's the principal who says: He talks, doesn't he? Why does he need speech therapy? It's the team who says, "We understand ASDs and our students make progress. We don't need more training." It's the teacher or parent who assumes that if the child is quiet and behaved in class (read: not disruptive), there must not be any issues, so why take the time and effort to do a sensory profile? Or the playground monitor who watches a student with autism "walk the fence" at recess, thinking he must be making a conscious choice to not join his peers; no need for social facilitation.

Just because the wheel doesn't squeak does not mean it is revolving effortlessly. Knowing that a child has been identified with an ASD should be enough to spark our curiosity about behaviors and reactions that are not typical, even when—especially when—those behaviors and reactions are not disruptive. Too often, this is the child who slips through the cracks, his disability invisible and therefore easily overlooked, never receiving the sensory and social communication services that will be so critical to his overall success—and to which he is entitled.

Complacency is a malaise, devoutly to be avoided. New information, new thought about teaching students with ASDs is being generated on an unprecedented pace. It's there and at the ready for teams wanting to work better, smarter and more effectively with this population.

Choosing reactive over proactive. Responding to problems only as they arise rather than anticipating and preventing them ultimately diminishes results for both you and your student. It is truly not the most efficient use of your teaching time or his learning time. Consider the difference between "survive" and "thrive."

17

Allowing anything less than a zero-tolerance policy on bullying and teasing. Good team dynamics demand that ALL members of the team guide each other towards appropriate behaviors by modeling healthy interactions. "'Typical' students often, if allowed to, reject the child who socializes or interacts differently," says Roneete. "It is critical that the teacher validate to the whole class each attempt the student with autism makes at socializing in his or her own way, placing the emphasis on what the student can do rather than what he cannot do. It introduces the reality to the class as a whole that in the real world, all people do not act similarly and that it is important to accept differences."

This is the way we do it. The spectrum nature of autism and related disorders automatically negates the idea that there can be a one-size-fits-all program or mentality for teaching students with ASDs. Yes—teaching students with ASDs is a measure more challenging. Commensurate results hang in the balance. When your student is young, it may seem like there is all the time in the world to work towards those results, but from a parent's standpoint, moments of truth arrive all too soon.

This Tale of Two Teachers occurred when my older son Connor was in his last years of high school. A student with ADHD, he never failed to produce above average work in homework, projects and class discussions. Tests were another story. Working with an outside education specialist during his freshman year, we were able to identify that the manner in which his brain stored and retrieved information was different than what a typical school test would demand. Because Connor did not meet the bar for an IEP, we were told to work things out with each individual teacher. And therein we discovered how vast can be the range of effort and attitude among teachers and their willingness to accommodate a different learner. One agreed to weight the homework more heavily than the tests. One offered extra credit projects to bridge the gap. One agreed to test orally. Some were unresponsive. Two were flat out belligerent. But in the end it came down to a microcosm of two teachers. I met with the first to explore what testing accommodations she could make for his learning differences. The response was "None. If he wants to go to college, he has to learn to take a test." He eked a C out of the class and that was the end of his career in that subject.

The second teacher, in just her fourth year of teaching, met my request for testing accommodation quite differently. "Whatever he needs is what we are going to do," she said. "I see no reason why he will not be successful in my class. And we are going to have a lot of fun too." And that is exactly what happened. He soared, chose to continue the subject in college, and at this writing is considering becoming a tutor in the subject.

Indifference will make a difference. But not the kind any of us want.

POISONOUS TEAM DYNAMICS

Combat mentality: the number-one deterrent to successful team building. Teacher or parent, a combative attitude on either side does not enhance our ability to make progress with the student with autism. Your relationship must be an alliance, not an adversarial face-off. You are all working in the same direction; your common interest is the child. It should never be about "me vs. you," or whether you like each other.

The Blame Game: undermining each other undermines your student's learning. Here's the fascinating point-counterpoint. Teachers want parents to know: communicating to your child that everything that is going wrong is the school's fault undermines your child's ability to trust me, to comply with necessary classroom boundaries, and ultimately, to learn. Parents want teachers to know: the behavior you are describing is utterly inconsistent with what I see at home, and therefore it is extremely hard for me to believe. How do I know that this behavior is my child's responsibility and not a reaction to someone else's unkindness or incompetence?

Oh, what a delicate line.

Don't put the child in the middle of this crummy tug-of-war. Whatever the situation, it can't always be his fault any more than it can always be someone else's fault. Teacher and parent must both step back and hear each other as objectively as possible when faced with information that makes your emotional level rise. Understand how common it is for children to exhibit a different set of behaviors at school than they do at home, and vice versa. And while your first reaction may naturally and understandably be defensive, know that most times, you don't need to offer an immediate response. It's okay to say, this is new information for me and I need to think about it and get back to you.

Failing to distinguish between assertive and aggressive. The difference between being assertive and being aggressive is usually the element of anger—and anger always has a cost.

- It costs us in trust.

- It costs us in potentially vital information. Teachers appreciate the parent who is a knowledgeable, effective advocate for their child, firm but respectful. That's light years removed from being a fist-pounder. Says one elementary school resource teacher: "In an ideal world, I want to share with the parent any inside perspective or 'off-the-record' knowledge I have about 'the system' and how they might navigate it to the benefit of their child. But if I sense in any way that the parent will use the information in a way that comes back on me or threatens my job, it is only natural that I will not share."

  This cuts both ways. Parents have told me: "I see teachers stubbornly clinging to methods that they claim have worked with other kids, but I know from experience it doesn't work with mine. I could save them a lot of wasted time and effort, but if I sense in any way that the school will use my information to try to cut future services, I have no choice but to remain silent. Meanwhile, my child doesn't progress at the rate he might otherwise."

- It costs us in lost learning time. A sixth-grade teacher agrees: "Time spent on procedural concerns translates into less time actually teaching. Combative parents mean I have to spend additional time anticipating confrontations, documenting my work beyond what is typical— covering my back, really—rather than engaging in activities that directly benefit the student:

teaching, preparing, researching, lesson planning, professional reading."

This too cuts both ways. "I dare not think about the hours I spend on phone calls, letters and meetings, trying to get our defiant school to comply with the requirements of the IEP," says one mom. "That's time I could be spending reading with my child, helping with homework, drawing, playing or even just talking with her—any of which would be more beneficial, to all of us."

Beneficial to all of us. That about captures it, wouldn't you say? Great teams do not just happen, they are built. I like to think of it as a tapestry in which we, the life-long learners and teachers, are the threads. Look at the back of any tapestry and you will see hundreds of colors, hundreds of threads of all lengths, many of their beginnings buried under other threads and their ends hanging, cut to size. All of us in it together, parents riding through eddies of programs, treatments and instructors, teachers tossed in a sea of children who seem to come and go with the annual tide. And the child himself—he's the one to whom it's actually happening, riding the whitewater of not only autism, but of many, many normal aspects of child development as well.

Yes, the back of that tapestry looks like an unruly mess. But turn it over to the front and the chaos vanishes. It's a thing of beauty, each stitch where it belongs; each stitch individual yet absolutely necessary to the whole. Far more than the sum of its threads, Team Tapestry crafts a work of art.

Chapter Three

I THINK DIFFERENTLY
Teach me in a way that is
meaningful to *me*.

My raised-on-ROM children don't know whether to be amused or aghast at how their parents grew up in an era without CDs, DVDs, cell phones or computers. My first computer predated Windows and used a revolutionary spreadsheet program called VisiCalc. Back in those frontier days, you either had an Apple MacIntosh or an IBM personal computer. The Macs and the PCs were Hatfields and McCoys. They not only didn't talk to each other, they couldn't talk to each other. They didn't "think" alike.

Your student with autism is like a Mac in a PC-dominated environment. He is hard-wired differently. Not incorrectly—just differently.

Macs and PCs couldn't communicate with each other because, bottom line, their operating systems were not compatible. Everything about Mac's architecture and command structure was different from the PC's. If you have been a lifelong PC-only or Mac-only user, you may consider yourself fairly computer-competent, and chances are you are not aware just how foreign it feels trying to navigate around the other system. I found out. During Bryce's third grade year with Jackie, I volunteered for a year-long project that involved transferring some of the kids' writings to computer files. Snap! I thought, I can do this at home in my abundant (winking here) free time. Then I was told it could not be done on my PC at home; it had to be done on Macs, in the classroom.

I'll spare you the details of the learning curve I never truly conquered. Week after week, I thought I had learned enough about the Mac operating system to do the project, only to run into new language or command obstacles. The project that was supposed to be enjoyable became a jaw-clenching exercise in anxiety. Why? Because fifteen years of day-in and day-out banging away on a PC had entrenched the Windows operating system so deeply in my gray matter that I was completely blindsided by how hard it was to put it aside, even temporarily, and learn to interact with a system that "thought" differently. My own "processing speed" slowed to a crawl.

Welcome to life as a student with autism, whose basic operating system is different from just about everyone else who is not on the autism spectrum. Macs and PCs made their debuts in the early to mid 1980s. Only recently have their incompatibility issues been resolved. Your student doesn't have twenty years. We need to adapt our teaching to his operating system, now.

No sugar coating here. Learning to relate to the autism way of thinking will be challenging because we have to be willing to step outside "normalcy." Collectively we are a social-driven society, all of us thinking and processing social and environmental inputs in a similar manner. Across all currents of life, our neuro-typical thinking patterns are naturally shared and naturally reinforced. To be able to truly understand a fundamentally dissimilar way of thinking requires you to suspend all you know and go somewhere you didn't even know existed. That takes courage. But that's where we must go if our goal as teachers is to be effective with our students with autism.

At the beginning of this endeavor is one critical distinction. This different architectural thought process has nothing to do with your student's abilities. We will never know the true extent of those abilities unless we establish communication via the architecture he has in place. The Apple Mac in Bryce's third grade classroom wasn't in and of itself incompetent or "challenged." The computer didn't fail, *I* failed to comprehend its operating system and input data in a format it could process. We must disabuse ourselves forever of the idea that our student with autism "could do it if he only tried harder." Also throw away the idea that all you have to do is "try harder." If we aren't trying through compatible channels, we can try until we cry and it won't ever matter. We have to try smarter, not just harder.

This difference in architecture impacts the skills embodied in what we call critical thinking (classification, comparison, application), executive management (attention, planning and memory functions) and social pragmatics (perspective-taking). These skills are missing from your ASD students' hard-wiring. But it is emphatically not true that they cannot be developed. Under patient and consistent instruction and coaching, children with ASDs can and do expand their social competence, improve executive functioning and achieve a functional degree of flexibility in thinking and conversing. Living proof of that is stomping around our upstairs bathroom right now, marinating himself in "man spray" and practicing lunchtime banter.

Books such as Dr. Temple Grandin and Sean Barron's *Unwritten Rules of Social Relationships* or the anecdotal insights of Jennifer McIlwee Myers recounted later in this book, offer up raw, eye-opening accounts of how children with autism or Asperger's Syndrome must navigate the journey to adulthood against strong current, up the fish ladder of the neuro-typical world. For some, the approach will be logical in the extreme, perhaps even to the point of appearing cold. For others their journey will be fraught with emotional turbulence, self-doubt and self-loathing, as they valiantly attempt to fit into society while inherently lacking the essential understanding of how to do so. No two ASD children are alike, but all their stories echo a common denominator: individual teachers had the power to make or break their will to stay the course and achieve.

HOW THINKING IS DIFFERENT IN AUTISM

At every turn in every day, we have the opportunity to help our student with autism understand our neuro-typical patterns of communicating and relating, and teach those skills that are so elusive to the autism way of thinking. Keep in mind always the spectrum nature of autism. While the traits that follow may be characteristic, they will vary widely in degree from mild to profound.

The One—and Only?—Learning Channel

Your student with autism has one-channel wiring in a polyphonic world. He likely processes most information via the one learning intelligence that works best for him; in most students with autism, this will be visual or tactile; less commonly, auditory. He struggles to process multiple sensory modalities. For instance, he can listen, or engage in movement activities, or talk, but he may falter when required to process more than one of these tasks at a time. It can be especially difficult to listen and write at the same time, or even to converse and make eye contact at the same time. The seamless integration among the senses that happens within the neuro-typical brain is missing in his brain.

Equally difficult is shifting back and forth between modalities (such as from visual to auditory and back again), and filtering out irrelevant sensory distractions: being able to distinguish the teacher's voice over the buzz of the flies on the windowsill, the garbage truck rolling by the window outside and the band practice down the hall. One-channel processing coupled with the inability to filter contributes to the ASD student's hyper-focused and repetitive behaviors. Constantly under a barrage of sensory chaos, he becomes physically, as well as emotionally, exhausted. Those single-focus or repetitive behaviors are calming and soothing to him.

A Zillion Parts in Search of a Whole

The neuro-typical brain thinks general-to-specific. Your student with autism thinks specific-to-general. Consider how acute that difference is. For him, each bit of information taken in exists in separate, discrete "boxes" in his brain. For us, bits of data naturally, effortlessly sift into categories and subcategories and sub-subcategories. Did you have to consciously learn that banana, apple, grapes and watermelon make up the category "fruit"? Bet you didn't; category "fruit" just made sense.

Our brain organizes the information we take in and even cross references it for us. Not so for your student with autism. Categorical thinking is difficult for him and must be taught. His brain is like a cavernous warehouse filled with bits of unrelated information. As his teacher, you need to help him learn to organize, label and associate all that information. It all begins with teaching the child to think in categories.

In the young child, the categories are few and unrelated. This is partly why your student will often respond with answers that relate only vaguely to the question. He has only a limited number of categories in which to slot the new information, and in his mind, it *has* to fit into one of them. His critical thinking ability will develop and expand over time if, as more information is taken in, he learns from us how to put it into categories. Those categories then become subcategories of other larger categories, and so on.

As you let this characteristic of the autism architecture sink in, you may—and should—find it overwhelming to conceive of every piece of information in your head existing independently of any other thought. What would it be like to have no ability to sort, to organize, to create associations? It's no wonder your student has difficulty learning. Wouldn't you?

Your student's inability to form categories has an equally formidable cousin: the inability to generalize information. As we've discussed, for the child with autism, every new experience exists in a vacuum. There's no "whole," no umbrella under which different-but-related ideas or experiences can gather. He does not generalize a new experience to prior experiences or knowledge, until he is taught to do so. If you teach him to safely cross the street at the intersection of Main and Smith Streets, that learning does not automatically apply to the situation that has him standing at the intersection of 23rd Avenue and Johnson Drive. To his way of thinking, it's not the same.

Teach him: to *categorize.* Start with simple, concrete categories like colors, clothes or vehicles and build to categories that are less concrete, like function, proximity or social categories like feelings. Explain why an object fits into one category or several, but not in others. Have him *compare and contrast* similarities and differences.

Teach him: *to apply concepts.* Help him understand that categories can represent concepts, and that information can be interrelated, that you can take what you know about particular situations and people and objects, and use it in other settings and situations.

Teach him: to *identify cause and effect.* Like information, the actions and reactions of people and objects don't exist discretely either. Relationships can be affected by choice. Start with simple, concrete examples and work up from there. If you leave your Hot Wheels out in the rain, they will rust. If you bop Alex, he won't want to play with you. If you ignore Erica, her feelings will be hurt. Actions elicit reactions and many of the consequences of his actions are within his power to control and affect. Teach him: isn't that great?

I Need to See It to Learn It

Many of your students with autism will be visual/spatial learners—they think in pictures rather than words. Your student with autism might tell you:

> *I need to see something to learn it, not just hear it. Words are frequently like steam to me; I know they are there but they evaporate before I have a chance to make sense of them. I need more time to process information than typical children. Information delivered in words comes and goes in an instant, and I*

don't have instant-processing skills. When information is presented to me visually, it can stay in front of me for as long as it takes to decode. Otherwise I live the constant frustration of knowing that I'm missing big blocks of information and expectation, and am helpless to do anything about it.

Whole Chunk Learning

Your student with autism may be a "gestalt" learner, absorbing information in chunks, rather than the more widely accepted, analytical step-by-step learning process. He watches and watches from the sidelines as other children pick up and perform skills and tasks he can't do. Then one day, he just up and does it. His language development may begin the same way, with echolalia (memorized "scripts" or whole blocks of language) rather than one-word-at-a-time learning.

Processing information in whole pieces like this compromises the child's ability to assign inferential meaning to the parts of the whole. He may be able to sing the "Star-Spangled Banner" or "O Canada," but have no concept of what a national anthem is. Unfortunately, today's academic curriculum is largely built upon an analytic learning structure—the very antithesis of optimal instruction to the child with autism who learns in a gestalt manner. Though not adequately recognized, gestalt learning is not a "lesser" way to learn. It is valid, it is acceptable, it is another way to learn.

Over and Over and Over Again

The behaviors of children with autism are frequently characterized by excessive selectivity and hyper-focus (rigidity and repetition). Their extreme dependence on routine and sameness is a result of a thinking architecture that has difficulty processing change. Even small variations from expectation—taking a different route to school, having a substitute teacher, changing the student's desks around, create cognitive chaos that can domino-affect the entire course of the day.

Our student with autism might explain it this way.

You may view my behavior and thinking as "rigid," but it's that way because sameness and routine are my life-lines to being able to handle the details of daily life that you take for granted. Knowing that parts of my day and my life will be the same every time helps me cope with the constant anxiety of living in a baffling world that seems to be in constant and unpredictable motion. I DO want to learn to interact with you and my surroundings. So please respect my fears and ease me out of my inflexibility gently, until I learn the skills that will make me more functional, and you learn the ways to adapt my environment so that I can learn. Within the safety of my comfort zone, create relevant, concrete, hands-on experiences that help me see and live the benefits of flexibility. Help me move out of that zone one baby step at a time.

Teach him: to think *flexibly and cohesively.* With thoughtful planning on our part that includes frequent, incremental opportunities for practice, he can learn to take life's little speed bumps without bottoming out. Where he is excessively selective and hyper-focused, teach him—through your words and actions—that

- there is more than one way to view a situation

- problems can have more than one solution

- ideas can be expressed and exchanged in different ways

- there is more than one "right" way to do most things

- there is meaning in communication beyond what we see and hear.

Teach him the power of having a Plan B or C or D, that problem solving is easier when we remember to ask "I wonder" questions and that knowing when to ask for help is just as important as getting the answer right. Teach him to expect unpredictability as part of life and social interaction and that it's not only necessary but can even at times lead to fun and unanticipated enjoyment.

A One-sided Coin

Your student with autism thinks in concrete terms. On its most basic level, that means he will interpret what you say in a very literal manner. Tell him to "shake a leg" and don't be surprised if he does just that. He's not being impudent—he's following your instruction. Metaphors, idioms and figurative language are not part of his mindset.

In the classroom this can result in difficulty with problems that ask the student to summarize or synthesize, or pick out the theme or main point. It affects the manner in which he is able to retrieve information: He might respond well to prompted retrieval, such as a multiple-choice or matching quiz. Difficulty skyrockets when he is faced with tasks entailing open-ended recall without aid of prompting or cueing.

On the more advanced level, his concrete thinking means that abstract concepts and groupings will be hugely difficult for him. Think of the game show *$25,000 Pyramid*. Your student with autism might be able to come up with categories such as zoo animals, types of trucks or foods that are vegetables—concrete subjects. But he would struggle mightily with abstract categories such as things that go around, things that make you sneeze, things that live in water. Or, even more nebulous: things that make you happy, things that are opposites, things that are luxuries.

Everyone Thinks Like Me—Don't They?

Perspective-taking abilities, or what professionals refer to as Theory of Mind skills, are notoriously impaired in your student with autism. Until they are taught differently, children with impaired perspective-taking assume that everyone in the world shares their same way of thinking, has their same thoughts about a person, event or situation, and shares their same points of view. That inability to generalize applies here, too. So, explaining a different point of view in one instance doesn't mean he understands that all people can have different ways of thinking in every different instance.

Perspective-taking is a social skill that involves knowing and understanding that the same words, events or objects may look, sound or feel different to different people. It is considering the thoughts, feelings, attitudes and beliefs of others before we speak or act. Many of the social/emotional gaps in your student with autism stem from this impaired perspective-taking. He can't anticipate what others might say or do in different situations, nor understand that what one person does in a given situation, another person may never do! Your student may not even understand that other people have thoughts and emotions, and thus he may behave in ways that come across as uncaring or self-centered.

Michelle Garcia Winner, a speech/language pathologist and veritable guru of teaching perspective-taking to individuals with ASDs, is the author of two monumental books on social thinking, *Thinking About YOU Thinking About ME* and *Think Social! A Social Thinking Curriculum for School-Aged Students.* Both are invaluable, and when I am Queen of Everything (a la Mary Engelbreit), I shall make them required reading for all teachers and parents. In her books, Winner defines the critical elements of perspective-taking as the ability to *actively consider* and *adjust to*:

- The thoughts and emotions of others as well as one's self, even if there is no direct interaction taking place

- Similarities and differences in religious, political and cultural beliefs of your own as compared to others

- Using prior knowledge and experiences as they pertain to communicating with others

- The motives and intentions of one's self and others, even if there is no direct interaction.

Without teaching these Theory of Mind skills, your student with autism may never experience the results and rewards of healthy perspective-taking ability detailed by Winner:

- To interpret the needs and wants of others

- To provide responses that are considered empathetic

- To safely navigate around persons who may have ill intentions

- To interact with nuance so that others do not perceive you to be too demanding or too straightforward

- To share in the passions or delights of others even without sharing the same level of interest in the topic purely because one can enjoy the underlying relationship that is evolving

- To engage in acts of socially related critical thinking and personal problem solving.

Teach your ASD student: that people have different ways of thinking, feeling and responding. That we not only respond to others but we initiate contact with others. That we share and reciprocate actions with others, not merely attempt to control our own situation. That we take social cues from others without imitating their exact behaviors and words. That we engage in cooperative and reciprocal give-and-take, not just parallel activity with others.

Remember that perspective-taking ability is unrelated to intelligence: having a high IQ or advanced language capabilities is not an indicator of perspective-taking abilities. In fact, Temple Grandin has observed that the children on the lower functioning end of the autism spectrum often seem to have a greater sense of perspective-taking.

And never, never forget: *he does not understand* the reactions his behavior produces in others.

START TO SEE THINGS DIFFERENTLY

Remember the old cliché, "everyone learns to put their pants on one leg at a time"? Bryce didn't. When he was learning to dress himself, he found it more expedient to sit on the edge of the bed, roll back, throw his legs up in the air and put his pants on both legs at the same time, all in one movement. He visualized it differently, applied a different motor-planning sequence, and came up with his own unique, efficient approach to a typical skill. The fact that 99% of the world puts their pants on one leg at a time doesn't make his way wrong, and in fact his way might even be better.

Teaching our children with autism will be an exercise in spitting into the wind if we are not willing to accept and respect that they think differently, then find effective ways to adapt our teaching accordingly. If we can't manage to be flexible in our own approach to teaching him, if we don't accept his basic mental functioning as valid and worthy of our effort, if we reject or disregard him at his very core level—we can't expect him to respond with any degree of motivation or desire to connect to us or our world.

The sweet spot is a meeting place somewhere in the middle. We shift our thinking enough to be able to teach to his way of thinking in a meaningful way. Then he can learn to be more comfortable with our way of thinking, and to feel competent in a neuro-typical world. Little by little the familiarity between us grows. Macs now communicate with PCs, and the dawning of the 21st century brought about the first annual Hatfields and McCoys Reunion Festival. There's never been a better time to learn to take that different perspective, to "think differently." You and your student will both learn things you never knew you never knew.

Chapter Four

BEHAVIOR IS COMMUNICATION:
YOURS, MINE AND OURS

Can we talk? Behavior is probably the most discussed, debated, dreaded and perhaps misunderstood issue within autism. It's the concern that has launched a thousand parent-teacher meetings and yet again as many medical and therapy consultations. It's the fire-breathing dragon, the Goliath, the T-Rex and the Titanic hitting the iceberg—sometimes all at once.

And yet behavior is a greatly weakened enemy once we accept a simple truth: that behavior never, ever comes out of nowhere. There is always an underlying trigger, an unmet need. Once we identify the trigger, we are three-quarters of the way to disabling it. Yes, it requires that we invest time and effort in sleuth work. We in the autism milieu sometimes refer to it as having to become a behavior detective, or a social detective. Before you start wilting at the thought of how time-intensive this approach might be, remember that the upfront investment of effort spent on behavior prevention pales to nothing against the draining, unproductive alternative of having to react over and over again to the same *preventable* behavior.

There are simple tools that make this job far less daunting than it seems. We'll head to the tool shed in a minute. But first, a prerequisite for using these tools: in trying to pinpoint underlying reasons for a child's behavior, we must first look at our own. We have to acknowledge that our own behavior is information we are imparting to the child about his environment. We can't question what his behavior is telling us without also questioning what our behavior is telling him.

I also urge you to be as gentle in your efforts to change your student's or child's behavior as you could reasonably expect of yourself. It strikes me as sheer lunacy how much we expect of our students with autism in the area of behavior modification when we as adults find it so difficult to accomplish ourselves. Every darn New Year's, out come the same tired old behavior-modification resolutions: lose weight, stop smoking, spend less money, exercise more. By the end of January, it's usually all over but the shouting. What real right do we have to expect greater inner fortitude of a child living with perpetual neurological challenge than we are able to muster ourselves?

The thing is, we frequently set ourselves up for failure because three or four New Year's resolutions are too many. We all know too well how demoralizing it is to swallow the fact that we didn't keep any of those resolutions, didn't manage to change our behavior. How much better it would be to pick one winnable battle at a time, to experience incremental success and the feeling of self-worth that comes with it before moving on to the next battle.

We can't hit on the answers to all behavior problems in one chapter of one small book, and we won't try. There are dozens of excellent books devoted solely to behavior management; you may have already read some of them. But this may be the first book you've read that focuses not just on the child's behavior, but in equal part on our adult behavior and the role it plays in the equation. Let's take a big-picture look at some factors that can influence behavior in the educational setting. Who better to explain his own behavior, and tell us how he perceives ours, than our child himself?

Our student with autism says:

- **Look for sensory issues first.** Many of my resistant behaviors come from sensory discomfort. The classroom is too bright, or too loud or there's too much on the walls to distract me. Maybe I need to sit closer to you; I don't understand what you are saying because there are too many noises in between—that lawnmower outside the window, Jasmine whispering to Tanya, chairs scraping, pencil sharpener grinding. Sitting in a chair may not be my best learning posture. My sense of equilibrium is such that I sometimes can't tell where the edge of the seat is—am I about to fall off? Maybe I could do my reading lying on a mat (full-length body contact is calming for me) or a beanbag chair, or leaning on a podium.

  Ask the school occupational therapist for sensory-friendly ideas for the classroom. It's actually good for all kids, not just me.

- **Provide me a break to allow for self-regulation *before* I need it.** A quiet, carpeted corner of the room with some pillows, books and headphones allows me a place to go to re-group when I feel overwhelmed, but isn't so far physically removed that I won't be able to rejoin the activity flow of the classroom smoothly. Or maybe I just need some movement—an errand to the office or a lap around the gym with my para or a peer buddy may be all it takes.

- **Keep a "behavior detective" log**. Keep simple running notes about when and where my troubling behaviors occur. Describe the activity and who's around at the time. Stop for a moment and try to become aware of the many sensory and social aspects of our surroundings. See. Hear. Feel. Smell. The things you may easily tune out may be the very things that are causing me discomfort, even pain. You are going to be amazed at how much this may reveal about the sources of my behavior.

- **Don't make a bad situation worse**. I truly don't mean to melt down, show anger or otherwise disrupt your classroom. You can help me get over it more quickly by not responding with inflammatory behavior of your own. Beware of these responses that prolong rather than resolve a crisis:

  — Raising the pitch or volume of your voice. I hear the shouting, but not the words.

  — Mocking or mimicking me. Sarcasm, insults or name-calling will not embarrass me out of the behavior. What it does teach me is that I can't trust you. It also teaches the class bullies new tricks to use on me when adults aren't within earshot.

— Making accusations you can't back up. If you don't have concrete proof that I did it, you are just guessing. What if you are wrong?

— Using what you call a "double standard." Forcing me to publicly follow a set of rules or expectations that are different from the rest of the class's rules not only makes it harder for me socially, it also squashes my self-esteem and affects my classmates' willingness to work with me as a peer.

— Comparing me or my efforts to that of a sibling or other student.

— Bringing up previous or unrelated events.

— Lumping me into a general category ("kids like you are all the same")

If you do fall into one of these, you can still produce a positive result by modeling how a responsible and compassionate person makes a sincere apology. I need to learn that everyone messes up sometimes, even you, and that even when the mistake looks huge, we can still make things right and move on.

· **If you are not getting through, try another way**. My mom chuckled, then looked sad when she read somewhere that the definition of insanity is always doing things the same way and expecting different results. If despite your repeated efforts, my behavior isn't changing, maybe the behavior that needs to change is yours. You have no idea how bad it feels to know that adults think my behavior is willful, that I could change my reactions to my environment if I just wanted to badly enough. It isn't, and I can't. You haven't found the root cause of my behavior yet; please keep looking! When teaching isn't working, the burden is on the teacher to change the teaching.

Author and speaker Jennifer McIlwee Myers recalls a childhood with Asperger's Syndrome and now, as an adult, still experiences its challenges. She has painful memories of a teacher who chose a mean-spirited approach to her behavior. That teacher missed enormous learning opportunities for a student who happened to learn differently. Jennifer tells this unvarnished story:

> "In third grade, I got in trouble during almost every vocabulary lesson. The routine was: we looked up the words in our dictionaries, wrote the definitions, then Mrs. Attitude (name changed to protect the guilty) went over the words with the class. The problem for me was, I loooooooove to read dictionaries. My nose buried in the dictionary, I didn't see or hear when she began talking to the class.... She would then call on me, and I wouldn't hear her. She would continue to try to get my attention from the front of the classroom (I assume—I never saw it) until she got more and more frustrated. She'd wind up coming over to my desk, loudly getting on my case and lecturing me. Every week.

> "Though it never worked, Mrs. Attitude thought that humiliating me in front of the class would

break me of this terrible habit. I really did hate being yelled at, and I really hated the extra ammo she gave the other kids so that they could increase their taunting on the playground. So I really did try. But handing me a dictionary and telling me not to get absorbed in it was equivalent to leaving an unwrapped Hershey bar on my desk and telling me not to eat it. But she assumed that I was driving her nuts on purpose. She seemed to have forgotten what the heck she was teaching. It was a vocabulary lesson! I was reading a dictionary! The fact that she didn't want me to learn new vocabulary words during the vocabulary lesson drove me up the wall!

"There were so many ways she could have dealt with this. She could have come over and tapped me on the shoulder before she started talking to the class. She could have set a timer with a loud bell on my desk and told me I had to close the dictionary when it went off. She could have kept me occupied writing definitions on the board while the other kids consulted their dictionaries. She could have coached me to help the other kids with their work. She could have assigned me work that didn't involve a dictionary. She could have ignored the problem and let me read the dictionary. She could have done a lot of things, but she didn't. She humiliated me for a behavior I couldn't control, and she made me loathe and distrust her for making my bullying situation worse."

- **Make sure your rewards are really rewards**. Being rewarded for good behavior with treats that I hate (ice cream hurts my teeth!) or toys I don't understand (glad YOU like the *Star Trek* Monopoly game) will not inspire me to change my behavior. My interests are very specific, and what gets my attention may be quite the opposite of what all the other kids might want. If you want to know what rewards I find motivating—ask me! If I'm not able to tell you these things, be alert for other signs that indicate what interests and encourages me.

- **Be the change you want to see in me.** Most (though not all) children with autism are mainly visual learners. I am going to believe what I see long before I absorb what I hear. If you yell, mock or hit when you are mad, I will too. If you are going to try to change my behaviors such as rocking, tapping or twirling, you can't expect me to absorb why I should do that while you're chugging all those Cokes or lattes, cracking your knuckles or your gum or jingling your keys. If you want me to learn to not interrupt and to pay attention to you when you talk, check to make sure you are giving me the same courtesy.

- **Choose one battle at a time**. "Multi-tasking" does *not* work for kids with autism.

- **Distinguish between behaviors that are harmful and ones that are just annoying to you**. Behaviors that affect my health or disrupt the classroom or home should be our first priority. Then please give some thought to other behaviors you find "inappropriate" or "negative." For instance, I'm sorry that it bothers you that I twirl my hair or the strap of my backpack. But of what real importance is it in the face of all I am...facing? Focus your one-thing-at-a-time efforts where they will have the greatest benefit, and while you are at it, remember what your attitude communicates to the rest of the class.

· **Be careful what you ask of me, or you might get it**. While children with autism do need constant social cuing, if you indiscriminately encourage me to be like the other children, you shouldn't be surprised if I swear, complain about homework and chores, cheat, bully, or sneak junk food. Or uglier. This is circular learning at its worst.

———

So now we have the assignment: behavior doesn't change until we find and address the root cause. Here, as promised, is the starter tool kit.

Functional Behavior Assessment, Functional Behavior Analysis

This is literally the ABC of behavior. It involves identifying the *antecedent*, or trigger, of the behavior, the *behavior* itself that we see the child display, and the *consequence* or result of his behavior. The assessment is part of the analysis. FBA can be anything from informal observation to detailed, quantified data collection. Either is best done alongside a person or persons trained in behavior analysis. Keep in mind the behavior equation we shared at the beginning of the chapter: Behavior = you + me + environment.

Sensory Profile

Occupational therapists will be familiar with the Sensory Profile, developed by widely respected OT Winnie Dunn. Parents/caregivers respond to 125 questions regarding the frequency/intensity of their child's responses to a range of sensory experiences. The results are scored by an OT, and can be invaluable in pinpointing environmental stimuli that may be contributing to behavior. Information brought to light by the Sensory Profile can also help your OT suggest modifications to the classroom that can help prevent disruptive behaviors.

Sensory Map / Sensory Diet

With the information gained from the Sensory Profile, an occupational therapist can design a "sensory map" and/or "diet" for the child. The map charts the child's day as he moves from activity to activity, identifies where sensory problems are likely to occur, and provides intervention suggestions, or diet. The diet acknowledges where sensory needs exist and provides suggestions for intervention. For children on the spectrum, the diet may need to include both calming and alerting activities. Disinterest and lethargy can be symptoms of sensory disorder just as much as hyperactivity.

Food Journal

Food can wreak all kinds of havoc with a child's behavior, far beyond the dismissive hyped "sugar high." Food allergies (disordered immune system response), food sensitivities (drug-like reaction to varying amounts of a food), low blood sugar, dehydration, vitamin deficiencies, absorption issues—the list is quite long. Keeping detailed notes on what and when the child eats alongside behavior notes can be very revealing.

Sleep Journal

Parents need to document the child's sleep habits at home. Chronic sleep shortage is a veritable prescription for behavior problems. Detecting the source of sleep problems begins with exactly the factors we've been discussing throughout the chapter: sensory issues such as household noise, uncomfortable bedding or night clothing fabric, smelly (to him) bath or laundry products. A child with proprioceptive needs might benefit from a weighted blanket or sleeping bag instead of sheets. And it should go without saying that television/computer activities right up until the moment of bedtime leave the child stimulated, not relaxed. Likewise, ix-nay on the caffeinated sodas or chocolate products any time during the evening hours.

A Clear, Fair and *Meaningful* Plan for Consequences

Your student's autism may be the reason (explanation or cause) for some of his behaviors, but it can never be the excuse (attempt to justify, perhaps without factual backup). No one would suggest that a child with autism always be spared the natural consequences of his behavior. But the huge qualifier here is: be very clear in making the connection between the behavior and the consequence. Keep your language simple and concrete and remember that visuals can be very helpful.

Jennifer again helps us recognize the gravity of this when she says, "We need to understand how our behavior can cause unwanted results for us. DON'T cut us too much slack when our behavior is potentially dangerous to us. For example, adolescent pre-stalking behavior should result in serious consequences—because not treating such behavior seriously when we are young can lead to problems involving law enforcement when we're older!"

Eyes and Ears—and Heart

Behaviors rooted in emotional triggers can be the toughest to detect, because your student with autism probably cannot readily identify his emotions. We really need to listen with our hearts, listen and look in places we can't easily hear or see. A child experiences many things outside our range of awareness—teasing, bullying, frustration, disappointment, ineptitude at a given task due to lack of ability or knowledge. All of these can erupt into behavior. And most critically—the child with challenged social-emotional and language skills will not be able to communicate what is wrong. The ongoing involvement of a speech language therapist is key. Art therapy can also be considered. Many children can express themselves through drawing, painting or sculpture when words are not possible.

If we can buy into the idea that learning is circular, it's only a short step further down the road to realizing that behavior too is circular. Like learning, its messages flow back and forth among the members of the team. Three centuries before the concept of autism emerged, Sir Isaac Newton described the behavior equation perfectly in his Third Law of Motion: for every action there is an equal and opposite reaction. This kind of built-up pressure is what launches that all-time favorite science project, the bottle rocket. Behavior issues can seem about that volatile! But you have control of this rocket's trajectory. Your words, your attitude, your actions and your reactions are determining factors in your child's environment and his response to it. Only when we take a clear-eyed look at our own behavior will we have a chance of positively impacting our children's.

Chapter Five

GLITCHED, GARBLED AND BEWILDERED
If we can't communicate effectively,
learning can't happen.

"Suppose you say that I said that she said something quite different; I don't see that it makes any difference, because if she said what you said I said she said, it's just the same as if I said what she said she said."

— Slow-Solid Turtle to Painted Jaguar in Rudyard Kipling's *The Beginning of the Armadillos*

I'll bet you were confused by the previous page. Maybe your first thought was to wonder if there had been some sort of printing error. But what if I told you there was no printing error, that there was a message on that page; that, in fact, the whitespace contained a blizzard of information, but that you simply weren't getting it? What if, as the author of this book, the "teacher," I chose to send the information in a form other than conventional words? Or what if I chose to write this entire chapter in the Kipling-esque double-speak quoted above? Chances are you would feel annoyed, possibly frustrated. Isn't it my responsibility as the teacher to provide information in a manner you can comprehend?

The answer is a resounding OF COURSE IT IS. It is our responsibility as teachers to do whatever is necessary to communicate effectively with all of our students. We may think we are doing exactly that, but the assumptions and expectations we carry as "typical" communicators fall far short of the mark with our student with autism. So very, very often, unknowingly but insidiously, we sabotage our efforts and theirs.

In plain, concrete terms, hear this: the student with autism *requires adaptive communication*. Many teachers are aware that children with autism are more often than not visual learners, and that they interpret language in a very literal, concrete manner. I addressed those two aspects of autism at length in *Ten Things Every Child with Autism Wishes You Knew,* and here I want to extend that discussion rather than repeat it.

Recognizing that our student with autism is a visual learner and concrete thinker is the tip of the iceberg. Like an iceberg, the characteristic language impairments of autism go far, far below the surface, and they make auditory language processing both treacherous and genuinely exhausting for him. Surrounded by typical contemporary conversation, our student is subjected to an impossible level of vocabulary, relentless use of vernacular, idiom, or just plain, I mean, like, ya know, sloppy use of the language and stuff. Layer on top of that the ephemeral nuances of language: vocal pitch, tone, volume and the sheer pace of talk (human and electronic) flying around your student with autism, and it becomes so indecipherable as to send him into self-defensive shutdown. It looks to you like he's not listening, but the reality is that *he* is desperately trying to comprehend but *we* are not communicating in a manner that makes sense to him.

Having to battle each day through a fog of what may sound to him like jabberwocky doesn't encourage our student to trust us as messengers. When communication falters or fails, so too goes his trust. And that trust is the glue that binds your relationship as teacher and learner.

> "I don't believe you!" said Painted Jaguar. "You've mixed up all the things (you) told me to do until I don't know whether I am on my head or my painted tail. And now you come and tell me something I can understand, and I don't trust you one little bit."

53

We may already be using a visual schedule for our student, or a choice board or some variation on sign language. We may have noticed their literal interpretation of language, maybe even find it somewhat amusing.

> Well-meaning neighbor: "My goodness, Justin, you are growing like a weed!"

> Justin: "You're a mean old man! My daddy pulls weeds and throws them away!"

That story came to me from a real mom, and I have a thousand of my own just like it. These incidents are humorous only in the moment, and not at all when you stop to consider that unchecked concrete thinking can lead to a lifetime of misinterpreting neighbors, co-workers and family members. How will that impact a child's ability to function as a happy, independent adult? I don't think many of us are really, really aware of how deeply disadvantaged our student with autism is in the area of communication, and how acutely aware of this we need to become in order to teach him in a meaningful way.

There's an interesting new culinary movement afoot these days called Slow Food. It's a backlash against the growing pervasiveness of empty-calorie, low-nutrient fast food. I'd love to see a similar movement applied to the use of language in communicating with our students with autism.

Slow down if you want to cultivate healthy communication with him. Move closer, speak to him directly (not calling from across the room), use low but intelligible tones. *Slow down.*

Cut out the fat. The empty-calorie, low-nutrient verbage such as slang, inference, sarcasm, allusion, exaggeration, cute but unnecessary plays on words. For him, these embellishments serve only to clutter and obscure, not enhance, the core message you're trying to put across. Use concrete, specific language.

Balance the diet. Just as any one food is not nutrition, words alone are not communication. Put all the team heads together to determine the types of visual and/or tactile supports and social language pragmatics teaching he needs. Actively teach him to understand body language, facial expression, vocal nuances. He will not "just pick it up" as he goes along. And it's not something we can relegate to social skills therapy he receives once a week (if at all). It requires perpetual integration. Every teacher, every setting, every day.

Give him adequate time to digest. It takes him longer to process and formulate the proper words to respond, and to motor plan whatever attendant behavior is needed. *Slow down.* Wait—many beats—before jumping in. Too often, we ask this child to pay the price for our own lack of time management skills. That's not okay. If his communication software calls for a five-minute warning or two-minute warning before an activity changes, build in a few extra minutes on your end to compensate, because this isn't special treatment. This is a system requirement.

Let him stop when he's full. Continuing to force-feed information past the point where he is able to adequately absorb it will only send his system into overload. As a result, you will see a blow-out or a shutdown, but either way, a "work stoppage."

FUNCTIONAL COMMUNICATION: MISSION ESSENTIAL

The importance of providing a child with a functional communication system, in whatever form it may take, cannot be over-emphasized. Here's an evocative scenario: imagine that your mouth is taped shut for an entire day. Your ability to contribute to conversations is severely compromised, as is your ability to ask for clarification of information that has whizzed by too quickly. It requires physical effort and exponentially more time to offer an opinion, ask for assistance, make your needs and wants known. You can't use the phone to summon help or expedite your tasks. Imagine further that any printed information handed you is written in symbols you don't fully understand. Verbal information is coming at you in a foreign language, you can only pick out every sixth word and maybe the ending verb—and that's only when the speaker slows down the pace of his speech, enunciates clearly and speaks to you directly.

In the face of these challenges, how long until you exhibited some "behavior?"

Now imagine this happens day after day, it is your *life*, not just some experiment.

And in imagining this, I hope you can begin to feel the great urgency and great poignancy in your ASD student's circumstance: language and communication is only one vital area of their lives with which they are struggling.

For nonverbal children and for early-verbal children, talk *is* cheap. Alternate and/or supplemental forms of communication are mandatory. Even for "high-functioning" children with autism who present as verbally competent, you can be certain of this: there are *always* holes and deficits, and they are deeper than you imagine. Even though my son is a teenager now—and is one of those kids with autism who presents as much, much more language-capable than he actually is—the extraordinary effort required of him and the toll exacted to execute competent social communication is actually palpable, and frequently heart-wrenching to have to watch.

Nobody sees me cry. Certainly not him.

As a society, we find it too easy to ignore or marginalize those who can't speak up for themselves, until they do something extreme that gets our attention. If we fail to provide a child with functional means of expressing his needs, we have no right to be shocked when he boils over with anger, frustration or grief. And it isn't enough that we provide him the means in finite settings; it must be a go-everywhere-he-does solution. The large visual schedule on the wall in the classroom is fine, the choice board on the refrigerator at home is fine, but what happens in the myriad venues outside the classroom and the home? The solution must be portable, something the child can use across all the landscape where his life is unfolding.

SPEECH IS NOT LANGUAGE IS NOT COMMUNICATION

The ability to talk, to form words, is only the mechanical beginning of verbal communication. Forming words is a function of the articulator muscles of the lips, tongue and face. Here's an analogy: you can switch on the ignition of a car and the engine will run, but without your steering and direction, an idling motor goes nowhere. At that point, it's a car but it's not yet transportation.

Merely using words does not equate to having a command of functional language, nor does not using words mean that communication is impossible. Functional language is comprised of receptive language (understanding what is being said to us) and expressive language (ability to make ourselves understood), all with the over-arching umbrella of social pragmatics. Functional language is not just words we say and hear, but how we say and hear them, when and to whom we say them and why we say them.

It's understandable that as verbal people ourselves, we tend to focus strongly on getting kids to talk. For parents of children who don't talk, it may be their single-minded goal. And yet, addressing the problem indirectly may be the shortest path, even if it seems counter-intuitive. New Hampshire physical therapist Patti Rawding-Anderson works with Easter Seals in offering social communication groups for children on the autism spectrum. She knows that parents worry that if they give their nonverbal child sign language or a picture system, the child will have no motivation to learn to talk. "But getting them to engage in their world is the most important thing. If you give them an augmentative communication system—a picture exchange system (PECS) is one example—or anything that allows them a sense of exploration and independence, and a FUN way to be successful, you will find that functional communication will follow."

KEEP IT CONCRETE: SAY WHAT YOU MEAN; MEAN WHAT YOU SAY

In America, our use of the English language is getting sloppier by the day. It's a wonder children with autism can understand us at all. They are forced to dodge language sinkholes every step of their day:

- Listen to any casual conversation today and count the number of times you hear "And I'm like..." when what the speaker really means is "And I said..." Or how about "And then he goes, like..." instead of "And then he said..." The child with autism is thinking, he goes? Where did he go?

- Listen to your own language. Is it littered with frightening idioms like putting a bug in someone's ear, opening a can of worms, or worse yet, suggesting that your restless student has ants in his pants?

- Do you assume your student understands homophones? Don't. Did he bat (verb) the bat (flying mammal) with the bat (baseball equipment)? Did the light from the light-yellow moon make it appear lighter than air?

- Beware phrasal verbs. You don't really mean he "burned up the track." You mean he ran very fast. He didn't really knock himself out on the math assignment, but he did work very hard.

- And then there's nonspecific (lazy?) speech. It's not fair to tell this student to "Go get it," with a glance over your shoulder, and expect him to understand that what you mean is "Use the atlas

59

on the top shelf to look up the capital of
Montana."

- Your student with autism does not infer like you
do. "You didn't turn your homework in" is merely
a statement of fact to him. He certainly doesn't
understand you are waiting for an explanation
from him, or for him to produce the homework.
He needs to hear what you want in the positive
rather than the imperative: "Please put your
spelling sentences on my desk." Don't make him
guess or have to figure out what it is you want him
to do. That's setting him up for failure.

At this point you may find yourself thinking that it's
rather grueling to have to police your language to such a
degree in order to communicate with your student with
autism. Now you begin to get some inkling of how
debilitating it is for him to have to deal with a whole world
full of "bullet train" chatterboxes who, to him, are
alternating back and forth between gobbledygook and
gibberish.

BE CLEAR ABOUT WHAT YOU ARE TRYING TO TEACH—AND TEACH ONLY ONE THING AT A TIME

Check your teaching materials against the challenges of
autism and you may find that they often confuse rather than
communicate, making it impossible to determine exactly
what the student does or doesn't know.

Your student's need for concrete expression extends into
the realm of words on paper. The print language your
student with autism confronts in textbooks, teaching

materials and tests can confound him every bit as much as the verbal chatter he hears. The following passage, adapted from my *Autism Asperger's Digest* magazine column, "Postcards from the Road Less Traveled," gives vivid example:

As the parent of a student with autism, I've become wary of anything with the word "standardized" in front of it. Standardized tests, lessons and worksheets—most require modification in order to be appropriate for a child with autism. "Math Suks!" warbles Jimmy Buffett's famous song. My son Bryce might agree, except upon closer examination, it's probably not math that "suks," but the confusing language in which it is sometimes presented and from which he is expected to learn.

Here is an example of how a "typical" math worksheet constitutes a veritable swamp of ambiguity for the student with autism. It will be an eye-opener to those who simply do not realize the depth and breadth of the language difficulties faced by so many ASD students. The example comes from an actual worksheet Bryce received on the first day of school one year. It nearly paralyzed him, and not because he can't add and subtract. With his moderate-to-severe language deficits (in vocabulary, inferential ability, lack of generalization skills), the worksheet, labeled as a Grade 5 math sheet, was a minefield of unnecessary and unclear language.

Addition and Subtraction

Directions: Add or subtract to find the answers.

Problem 1: Eastland School hosted a field day. Students could sign up for a variety of events. 175 students signed up for individual races. Twenty two-person teams competed in the mile relay and 36 kids took part in the high jump. How many students participated in the activities?

- "Students could sign up for a variety of events": unnecessary, irrelevant information

- 'Twenty two-person teams.' Bryce read this, as many ASD students would, without the hyphen: 22, not 20 x 2. The directions tell him to "add or subtract to find the answer," but the text shifts in mid-problem, requires multiplication within the add-or-subtract operation. Unclear, inconsistent directions are nearly impossible for many ASD kids to follow.

- We don't really know how many students "participated" because some "competed" and some "took part," but some only "signed up."

- The worksheet is labeled "Grade 5," but the Flesch-Kincaid Readability test rates this problem as Grade 9.

The same problem rewritten in an autism-friendly manner that emphasizes math, not language might read: **At Eastland School field day, 175 students ran in individual races. 40 students ran in a relay race, and 36 kids did the high jump. How many students participated in field day?**

Problem 2: Each school was awarded a trophy for participating in the field day activities. The Booster Club planned to purchase three plaques as awards, but they only wanted to spend $150. The first place trophy they selected was $68. The second place award was $59. How much would they be able to spend on the third place award if they stay within their budgeted amount?

- In the first sentence, reference is made to a "trophy." In the next sentence, it changes to "plaque," then it's back to "trophy" and in the fourth sentence it becomes an "award." All are referring to the same thing, but the math problem has now become an exercise in synonyms, obscuring the math intent.

- Problem assumes an 8th grade vocabulary. How many children know what a "Booster Club" is? A club for people who need baby seats at restaurants?

Autism friendly wording: **A group of parents had $150 with which to buy trophies for the teams finishing first, second and third place. The first place trophy they selected was $68. The second place trophy was $59. How much money was left to spend on the third place trophy?**

For the child with autism, these problems do not assess math skills, they evaluate ability to decode the language of a poorly written standardized worksheet designed for a general population, one written at several grade levels above both the student's chronological age and even the purported grade level of the worksheet itself.

I want you to know that I fully realize that, even when you are able to comprehend the magnitude of this problem, figuring out what to do about it may seem overwhelming. After one such session I had with one of my favorite teachers, she said: "I completely understand what you are telling me about the fact that he thinks differently. In order to accommodate that, I can see that I would have to go through all my materials and revamp everything for him. Frankly, I just don't see how I can manage that—I have 150 students. What can we do?"

Her approach was the right one, teamwork in action. She acknowledged a very real and large problem and I acknowledged very real and large constraints on her time. Her suggested solution was to pull Bryce into a three-way meeting and let him know that homework was to be interpreted by the spirit, not the letter of the assignment, and that she was giving permission for Mom to be the arbiter of that. We could write, we could discuss, we could draw, we could look at the Internet—whatever made the information comprehensible to him, and I would sign off on what we had done. This approach had the added advantage of forcing Bryce to think flexibly—and many times that was more difficult than the assignment itself! On the other end, she modified her assessment methods to ensure that he was truly able to communicate what he knew. Along the way, the school speech therapist would step in with particularly difficult assignments, using her sessions with Bryce to break down things down into understandable pieces.

I have one of those sneaking feelings that you may end up thanking your student with autism for pushing you to examine your printed materials more closely. We may go along for quite a while using materials that we think are working until one day we get eye-popping evidence that they aren't. I'm thinking of a social studies worksheet we encountered asking students to locate the USSR—on a 21st-century map. Bryce knocked himself to bits trying to find a republic that had already ceased to exist before he was born. Assuming a level of prior knowledge—that he would know that the bulk of the former USSR is now called Russia—is just as unfair to the student (any student!) as are poorly written materials.

BEYOND WORDS

By focusing so heavily on the speech components of communication, diction and vocabulary, it's easy to overlook the aspects of social communication that are less concrete and admittedly much harder to teach. Because your student with autism experiences language in its most concrete form, he will need a great deal of guidance and an even greater amount of practice to move beyond his concept of using language merely as a tool to get needs met or get information. The vast scope of *communicative intent* is not automatically present in the consciousness of children on the autism spectrum. These are complicated facets of communication that go far beyond diction and vocabulary: that people use words to comfort, to praise, to entertain, but also to provoke fear, shame and trickery.

At age three, Connor would burst into his grandparents' house three times a week with the greeting, "B-i-i-i-g TRUCKS!"and at age four, "I got a dinosaur!" was Bryce's standard greeting. It took patient preschool teachers some months to instill the understanding that we say "Good morning" when we come into class or see someone for the first time that day. That's the beginnings of social pragmatics—the social use of language—and for the student with autism spectrum disorders or ADHD, it only gets even more complicated. Asking, greeting, negotiating, protesting, instructing—these tend to be verbal tasks or expectations.

Beyond that level lies the realm of nuance, inference and nonverbal communication with all its explosive potential for misinterpretation and social misery.

There are three broad categories of social communication, all of which are minefields for the child with autism.

> **Vocalic communication:** He doesn't "get" the nuances of spoken language: sarcasm, puns, idioms, hints, slang, abstraction. He may speak in a monotone or he may speak too loudly, too softly, too quickly or too slowly.

> **Kinesthetic communication:** He doesn't understand body language, facial expression, emotional responses (crying, recoiling). He may use gestures or postures inappropriately, or miss the communicative intent of eye contact.

> **Proxemic communication:** He doesn't understand physical space communication, the subtle territorial norms of personal boundaries. He may be an unwitting "space invader." The rules of proxemics not only vary from culture to culture, but from person to person depending upon relationship: Intimate? Casual but personal? Social only? Public space? For most ASD kids, deciphering proxemics requires an impossible level of inference.

STUDENT SEE, STUDENT DO

Your very visual student with autism depends on you to model the kinds of behaviors and responses you want to see in him. Show, in addition to telling him, what you expect of him, and do it repeatedly and patiently and in a manner that makes sense to him.

And above all, show him some basic respect. Acknowledge that the times when he is angry, distraught or overwhelmed are not times when he is going to be receptive to teaching. Would you be, even as an adult? If during these moments we employ raised voices, scorn, annoyance and/or castigation, the only thing we will be teaching him about functional communication is that language can be wielded to inflict hurt.

Teaching this daunting but rich complexity of language and communication cannot be laid in the lap of a speech therapist who sees the student for a couple of half-hour sessions a week. Nor can we compartmentalize the teaching of language skills separate from social skills. They are inseparable and omnipresent. For your student with autism, this means that there is challenge in every waking moment, yes, but there is also opportunity present at every turn in every situation. The teaching of functional language must truly become an ensemble effort, every teacher in the child's circle of learning using these innumerable teaching moments to move toward a very life-changing goal: the student arrives at the understanding that language in its most basic form will not only get his needs met. More than that, in its most glorious and elevated form, it will give him the power to define himself as he wants others to see him, and to stake claim to the place he rightfully wants to occupy in the world.

Now we're talkin'!

Chapter Six

TEACH THE WHOLE ME
I'm much more than a set of "broken" or "missing" parts.

"The whole is more than the sum of its parts." Most of us recognize Aristotle's famous truism. But he went on to say more: that "educating the mind without educating the heart is no education at all." Aristotle, both philosopher and scientist, understood this inescapable connectedness between all the parts of ourselves. Within that interconnectedness lies the potential for either soaring harmony or soul-shattering discord, depending on how each part works in relation to the others.

And, "parts" is what we too often come to see in our students with autism. We focus on the symptoms of autism to such a degree that we lose sight of the child as a holistic being. A child with autism is not a malfunctioning engine to be "parted" out and repaired; the speech therapist fixes the talking part and the sensory and fine motor part goes to the occupational therapist. A physical therapist deals with the gross motor part. This part goes to the behavior specialist and this part to the psychologist and the dietician, and so on. All of these disciplines are invaluable pieces of the whole puzzle. But unless actively integrated with each other, they can actually escalate the very obstacles we are striving to remove. "We should not 'therapize' children," says Patti Rawding-Anderson, "filling their world with all different adults who are trying to do something to them. What message does this send the child? More important than therapy, language and cognition is to help the child see the inter-relatedness of the people in his life, and build upon those relationships across various situations. If a child feels connected, he will have the internal motivation he needs to pursue the other things."

When we don't create that connectedness for the child with autism, one of the gravest risks we run is mistaking compliance for learning. You can get a child to perform certain behaviors or bring forth certain words in certain situations. But without addressing the core reasons for the original behaviors, or conveying the function and utility of language and communication, the child is still without meaningful context.

Speech is only one of the many building blocks of communication; rote repetition of manners doesn't equate to social understanding; and attempting to change behavior without looking at underlying biomedical, sensory or emotional triggers simply isn't looking at the whole picture. It therefore will never be a whole answer, never result in a whole child or an adult able to do much more than go through the motions of social expectation. You may have put out the fire, but in its place are opaque puddles.

How successful we are in teaching the whole child has a lot to do with our own personal "culture of disability." Service providers like Patti work with a wide spectrum of families and teachers, and these professionals tell you it's almost eerie how individuals who come to them for help sift into two camps. Ask these two camps the same question: tell me about your student or child. In the first camp are teachers and parents who say: "This child is so bright and energetic! He loves the outdoors and he has a lot of knowledge in his head. How can we help him settle and focus better so he and his classmates can enjoy each other?" From the second camp, we hear: "This child is disruptive and inattentive. He's always making noises, making messes, getting out of his seat and talking out of turn. He needs to get himself under control."

It's pretty clear which of these attitudes is more "whole child," which teacher is going to build the more successful teacher-child relationship, and which teacher's student is going to be the more successful learner and ultimately the more successful adult.

We've already acknowledged that autism is an extremely complex condition, not to mention being a spectrum condition along which every individual—and their teachers and parents—occupies a unique spot. It may be easier to see the whole child in your student with autism if we step back and look beyond what autism is to look equally hard at what autism isn't.

- **Not everything she does is a result of her autism**. All human beings have innate personalities; your student with autism also has aspects of her individuality that manifest apart from her autism. Children with autism are not the only ones who shave the kitty or eat dog food on a dare. His single-minded passion for running, reading or ham radio isn't necessarily autism-driven. Both are aspects of a developing child who is pushing the limits on one hand and discovering his own assets on another hand. Autism may affect the degree to which these behaviors manifest, but is not always the reason for them.

- **Natural "typical" development will be happening as well.** During his school years from pre-K through 6th grade, Bryce earned a consistent reputation as a cheerful, tireless workhorse. So I was very surprised, at mid-7th grade, to have a teacher tell me, not at all unkindly, that he "fusses and complains all the time." When I repeated the "compliment" to him at home, he beamed and replied, "Yes, I do! I'm a teenager!"

The teacher knew that his behavior was part of adolescence, not autism. It is also "typical" and "normal" that a teenager might care more about a peer's opinion of him than he would a teacher's. A slightly more subdued Bryce came home shortly after the fussing-and-complaining conversation and asked me if I remembered Denise, a girl who had gone to grade school with him but had moved away with her family a few years back. I did remember her as a nice girl, so I was happy for Bryce when he told me she had moved back to town and was again in some of his classes. He hesitated just a beat, then told me: "She says I have changed. She says I used to be nice but now I'm kind of grumpy." I asked him, do you think that is true? Well, he replied, yes, I guess it is—in a way, sometimes. But I could see the wheels turning. Maybe the stereotypical grumpy teenager is an amusing way to treat a teacher. But maybe it isn't the best choice of personas to present to a friendly member of the opposite sex. Shortly after this incident, we saw a change in his behavior. The good-natured Bryce started showing up more and more frequently again.

As his teacher: Emphasize commonalities, not just differences that many children with autism share with their "typical" peers.

- They have dreams of the future. Many aspire to grow up, to have a job, a home of their own, money of their own, to drive a car, to marry, to have kids.

- They enjoy humor and fun. If you think your student with autism appears to have no sense of humor, stop a moment to consider just how subjective humor is. Americans sometimes think British humor odd, and vice versa. Older folks aren't amused by what passes for humor with younger folks. The joke that entertains some mortally offends others. Humor is in the eye of the beholder. Your student with autism most assuredly has a sense of humor—it just may not be the same as yours or his peers. What a great opportunity!

- They can and will be friendly and sociable—in their own, appropriately calibrated way. The spring pep rally or the crush of the Halloween parade may send your student with autism into sensory overload, but the three-person Lego Club group or a two-person sandcastle team may be just right.

- They can belong. It's only a matter of tailoring the setting. Team expectations such a baseball, basketball, lines in a play or a band solo may overwhelm, but there are many ways to be part of a team without the undue pressure all-eyes-on-you of personal performance. Swim and track teams are generally more personal-best oriented than group team sports. Singing in the choir, painting the scenery for the class play or taking photos at school events are endeavors that are ideal for all-comers. Volunteer opportunities at places like pet shelters and food banks draw the child into a larger world.

· *They have feelings.* Having open communication with a child with autism about feelings and emotions can be difficult. Conversation in general is difficult for them, and being able to identify feelings is more difficult yet. That they may not be able to show or communicate their feelings does not mean that they do not experience the full galaxy of human emotions. If we are to be able to help them recognize, empathize, identify the feelings of others, it must start with our validating that the same feelings live within them.

· They want to be liked and have friends—just like everyone else. If you've ever yearned to do or learn something but simply didn't know where to start, you'll understand where the child with autism stands. Social communication requires an intricate set of skills. Your student with autism doesn't have them—which is in no way the same thing as not wanting to have them.

As his teacher: Recognize when outside help is needed, or when the school or teacher, hard as they may have tried (or not), simply isn't a good fit. This is where it is incumbent upon the team to look at the whole child in the whole picture, remove egos and "should haves" from the equation, and make decisions that are in the best interests of the child.

Giving up that ego can be hard. Happily, I have by now had enough firsthand experience doing it that I can see the value and the remarkable end results of letting go. Acknowledging that you or the school can't provide the appropriate and necessary services for this particular student with autism is not failure—it is the very essence of putting the needs of the child first. When done in the true spirit of wanting the child to succeed, it is courageous.

Letting someone with a different skill set and a "clean slate" tackle the situation is often just the ticket. I went through a years-long, painfully unsuccessful process of trying to teach Bryce to ride a bike. It turned out to be a microcosm for many whole-child learning lessons, and I will talk more about it in Chapter Nine. But here, I can tell you that the happy ending to the story had everything to do with my conceding that I was not the right one to teach this skill, and that the harder I tried, the more it didn't happen. Our adapted PE teacher, Sarah Spella, volunteered to take over the job—and accomplished it in under an hour.

The critical component was my being able to let go of ego. Maybe I "should" have been able to teach him to ride a bike myself—I had taught Connor, my older son, on a "normal" timetable. But with Bryce, I had reached the point where accepting outside help was the only scenario that made sense. My failure would not be in my lack of success in teaching him to ride the bike, it would be in neglecting to look beyond my ego for the resources to achieve the goal.

It takes courage and initiative, says Sarah, to be able to say, "I think my student or child can do this, but I am not the right one to teach him. I may not be teaching him the way that he needs to be taught." Bryce learned to ride a bike because every subconscious expectation had been removed. Alone in the gym with Sarah, he was away from the prying eyes of neighborhood children who might snicker at his training wheels, away from a parent who he knew had successfully taught an older sibling at a much younger age. He was away from the specter of the other bikes in the garage poised for the annual vacation, away from having to worry about "being brave" if he fell.

"Be aware of how much information kids get about themselves from their environment," Sarah told me. The measuring stick is never far away from a child, whether in the form of a spoken expectation, "You can do this" or those unspoken expectations all around them, like seeing the six-year-old riding without training wheels. As teachers and parent-teachers, part of our job is to recognize how the educational setting is affecting the child, how it may be impeding learning and when it's time for a change.

Respecting your ASD student as a complex but complete self must be a concept as circular as all the others we discuss in this book: whole child, whole teacher. Accept and respect your own developmental timeline. "We think about the developmental sequence for the child," says Patti Rawding-Anderson, "but parents (and teachers) go through a developmental sequence too. You're not just born with the skills and knowledge to parent or teach a child who has challenges. It's a parallel process you follow with the child. Too many 'systems' don't take this into account—the need to nurture your own development as you build a relationship with the whole child."

"The whole is more than the sum of its parts." Today we have a new word for Aristotle's axiom: synergy, from the Greek word *sunergos*, meaning "working together." Whatever we call it, only when we take to heart and put into practice this 2,300-year-old-wisdom will we truly be able to say that we have left no part of this child behind.

Chapter Seven

BE CURIOUS
...be very curious.

*"Curiosity is the very basis of education and if you tell me
that curiosity killed the cat, I say only the cat died nobly."*

-Arnold Edinborough

Amid several thousand years' worth of knowledge humankind has amassed about the workings of the human brain, autism is quite the new kid on the block. The word "autism" didn't even exist before the work of Dr. Leo Kanner in 1943. As such, we are standing very much in the pre-dawn half-light of understanding. We can all admit that autism is yet a puzzlement to most of us. We can also admit that each of us confronts that which we don't understand in our own way. Some people embrace the unknown as collective potential—a means to knowledge and a challenge not only acceptable but exciting. Others will avoid such mystery, seeing it as ultimate chaos.

I'm guessing that most who choose to become teachers gravitate towards the first group: life-long learners, knowledge-seekers comfortable with taking on a certain level of risk. Most teachers I know would look at their student with autism with a real desire to reach this enigmatic child and make a difference in his life. We parents often tell our best teachers that they "really lit a fire under" our child. But how do you strike the spark for a child who outwardly seems remote, detached—unknowable?

In your role as firestarter, and for your student and you as a team, curiosity must become both the flint and the fuel. Inquisitive thinking, that endlessly questioning spirit, is the basis of all human progress. "Inquiring minds want to know!" blares the old tabloid newspaper ad. Typical young children embrace this. They ask and ask and ask about their world, until they wear us out with their questions. The more curious of my two kids asked me, do farts weigh anything? The lady is fat because she has a baby growing inside her? How did she swallow the baby? How come people don't fall off the bottom of the world? If an orange is called an orange, why isn't a banana called a yellow? If the shampoo is green or purple or orange, why are the bubbles always white? Is a skeleton a person?

Did you know that Einstein actually said, "It is a miracle that curiosity survives formal education"? If I were an educator, I would *dive* to pick up that gauntlet! And never will there be a child for whom it will be more important to cultivate curiosity than for your student with autism.

Your student with autism never had that typical child-curiosity to lose. The exercise of curiosity requires a certain level of risk-taking, that metaphorical stepping off the path, trading what you have in hand for what's behind Door #1. That is just too tall an order for the student with autism; the world he experiences may be literally (given sensory dysfunction) and figuratively too uneven to consider such boldness.

Typically-developing young children, with emerging self-reliance, are much freer to indulge their naturally curious natures because their lives are filled with experiences that are mostly positive. Unencumbered by the hell of half a dozen disordered sensory modalities, effortlessly processing the simultaneous inputs that come their way, able to relate to people who think more or less like they do, most of their experiences are not just positive, but stimulating, fun, useful. They are able to roll with the little nicks and bruises to knees and feelings that come along the way because the balance is in their favor. The return they get for their investment in curiosity pays worthwhile dividends.

I've already suggested in several different parts of this book, and let there be no question about it: for your student with autism, the world is often not a delightful place. Although he may gather encyclopedic knowledge in one or two specific interest areas, there is no general sense of wondering or questioning that drives him to want to explore every little new animal, mineral or vegetable that crosses his path. For him, the balance may not be towards positive experiences. He's working really hard just to stay upright and put one foot in front of the other on a slender path already booby-trapped with tree roots and potholes. Too often, new experiences defeat rather than reward him. *Be curious?* he says. *There's more than enough already pulling and pushing me off balance as it is. Why would I volunteer for more turmoil?*

For this student, the art of asking questions may come only after long, patient instruction, encouragement and practice. Especially difficult will be the "I wonder" questions which demand so much more of him than a factual response. But without a foundation of curiosity, his world will remain two-dimensional and without that figurative shower of cerebral sparks that makes learning such a dynamic experience, over and over again. It's time for you to invoke all that led you to become a teacher in the first place—to instill the thrill of discovery, to become utterly bewitched by the vastness of knowledge and all the possibility it embodies.

When Bryce was very young, I couldn't even coax him to be curious about Curious George. He was always out the door before I even got as far as "George was a good little monkey and always curious...." He rejected not only George but nearly all typical children's books, and that made me intensely curious and determined to find the inroad. Eventually I did—he didn't like stories about animals. He wanted stories about kids.

It took a heroic amount of curiosity-driven trial-and-error, but I learned to stir his curiosity in new experiences by going in through the back door of his narrow interest areas. He resisted our annual trips to the apple orchards until I told him he could soak himself in the rotary-head sprinklers (he loved any kind of water play) or he could splat the fallen rotten apples against the tree trunks (made cool sounds and looked like barf). Score!

Ultimately, his potentially traumatic transition to middle school was smooth as silk—because he had a teacher who was pretty darn curious. This teacher said, I really want to know how to connect with him. I'd like him to make me a list of every movie he's ever seen, so we can talk about all kinds of topics. What has worked for him in the past? What hasn't worked for him in the past? Tell me anything about him that you think is important for me to know.

It does take effort and initiative to be curious yourself, and curious enough to step inside the autism way of thinking to see what might make your student curious, too. The job will be much, much easier if you wipe your slate clean of any and all preconceived assumptions you may harbor about your student, perhaps not even consciously. Never assume anything! Assumptions without facts behind them are only guesses, and preconceived notions will squash both your curiosity and your student's as surely as the famous short film "Bambi vs. Godzilla." An old proverb tells us, "Who shall kindle others must himself glow." To kindle curiosity:

- *Remember* that autism is an open-ended equation, one that should never end with our deciding that the child has reached "the extent of his capability."

- *Forget* using teaching tactics not aligned with the autism architecture of thinking: *wonder* how well strategies you've always used with typical students will fare within the structure of autism. Be willing to change up what you've always done.

- *Remember* that teaching this uncurious child the love of learning itself is far more imperative than any facts you may want him to learn.

- *Forget* comparisons to other students, even other ASD students. This one occupies his own singular spot on the autism spectrum.

In urging us to be curious and assume nothing, our child could illuminate the hundreds of ways in which we might go awry with seemingly benign assumptions:

If you don't get why I don't get it, back up and ask "I wonder...?"' I may not know or understand the rules, or the reason for the rule. Am I breaking the rule because there is an underlying cause? I know I'm not supposed to get out of my seat without permission, but maybe I've tried and tried to get your attention and failed. Are your rules contradictory? We are not supposed to eat in class but you hand out candy when we do well on the spelling test, so why can't I get my apple out of my backpack?

I may have heard your instructions but not understood them. Or maybe I knew it yesterday but can't retrieve it today—my rote memory is great; my free recall ability, not good. Are you sure I really know how to do what you are asking of me? Be curious! Why do I suddenly need to run to the bathroom every time I'm asked to do a math sheet? Maybe I don't know how or fear my effort will not be good enough. Stick with me through enough repetitions of tasks and skills to where I feel competent. I can learn and I will learn, but I need more practice than other kids.

I know you want me to learn facts, but before I can do that, I need to learn to become comfortable with the process of learning itself—and that takes curiosity!

You may not know all the answers right from the start. Be curious enough to say, "I don't know, but I'll find out." Asking for help from someone who knows more than you do is the mark of a strong teacher. It sets the best kind of example of all for me.

Tap into your old childhood skills. Ask and ask and ask— ask the occupational therapist, even if the problem doesn't appear to be sensory or motor related (never assume!). Ask the speech pathologist, even if it doesn't appear to be language related (never assume!). Ask your student himself, even if you think he won't be able to give you the answers— never assume! *Be curious* enough to ask classmates and siblings, because you don't know what goes on in the restroom, the locker room, the back bedroom, the back yard and every other nook in this wide world where the child is out of your earshot and line of vision. The insights of a child may be strikingly different than those of an adult. Ask the "I wonder" questions, and ask them of the range of professionals, paraprofessionals, family members, caregivers and peers. Here is where circular learning can rise to its highest level, and where teamwork is at its most effective.

"I wonder...?" Such an empowering approach, suggesting so much more possibility than merely asking "why." Can't you just picture our child and his speech teacher with their books and their wonderings—partners in learning, gently pushing boundaries. It's so telling, and so appropriate, that the word "wonder" has two meanings: 1) to question, and 2) to marvel.

Chapter Eight

CAN I TRUST YOU?

Champions and advocates come in all shapes, sizes and persuasions, but I never pictured one who would cheer my efforts on with a cry of "Good on ya, mate!" Australian by birth, American by choice, Nola Maureen Flanagan Shirley ("that's my name; use all of it!") was one of the most influential people in Bryce's life. We met Nola back in Chapter One; she was Bryce's paraeducator for three years. After that she became a member of our family and I of hers. Her relationship with Bryce was pure karma: they arrived at Capitol Hill School on the same day in 1997, both assigned to a new developmental kindergarten classroom. They left for good on the same day in 2004, she to retirement and he moving on to middle school. We stood on the sidewalk in front of the school, together there for the last time on an afternoon in June and I thought: he looks so grown up since that first day, and she looks exactly the same to me. How does that work? No time to ponder; he's flying down the walk, shirttails aloft on the breeze. He's not running away from us; he's rushing delightedly, confidently, to discover the next phase of his life.

During the years Nola guided Bryce, she wrote home to me every single day in a school-home communication notebook, so I thought I had a good picture of what daily life in the classroom was like for Bryce. It was only some years later, with the perspective of hindsight that I became more and more curious about the minute-by-minute construction of the concrete (like his thinking) foundation she had built under him. During a long conversation on her homey back deck, the big picture unfolded.

I asked her: how was it that she was so successful with Bryce? The answer came without hesitation. Well, she said, that's pretty simple. He trusted me.

That's pretty simple. He trusted me.

Doesn't that come close to being oxymoronic? It's an uncomplicated statement, but for most people, trust is surely one of the most complex and risk-laden of human relationships. For someone with autism, it is even more so.

Where did that trust come from, I asked her; how did you build that trust? And her reply: "Bryce trusted us because we didn't tell him he had to do something—we showed him what good things could happen if he did." He learned that doing what was asked of him had consequences he would enjoy. "And," she added, "I never asked him to do something I wasn't doing myself, whether it was mixing finger paints, going to Field Day, or cleaning up the science experiment."

Time and again throughout the morning on that sunny porch, our conversation boomeranged back to that core of trust. And boomerang is the proper metaphor, an Australian weapon—but let's call it a tool—"designed to return to the person who throws it," according to the dictionary. What was that boomerang gathering on its journeys before it elliptically returned to her?

Respect.

The bricks of Bryce's trust in Nola were composed of her uncompromising respect for him and the way he saw the world. Each demonstration of respect strengthened the team foundation under them. The result was a self-confident child who was able to venture out of that world of self, attempt new experiences, rise to social and academic challenges, take calculated risks despite the obstacles his autism presented. Bryce's day was a roadmap guided by Nola's respect for his very specific, classic-autism needs. The short list looks like this:

She respected his need for:

- Predictability and routine

- Feeling like he had a choice, not backed into a corner, put on the spot or dictated to

- Visual cueing

- Personal space and accommodation of his tactile defensiveness and other sensory issues that interfered with learning

- Extra time to acclimate or prepare for a potentially difficult activity.

Our student with autism likely knows nothing of French philosophy or Rene Descartes' "I think, therefore I am." But if he could paraphrase, he might say:

I trust, therefore I can.

Trust is the very foundation of learning, not an add-on. Your student with autism must interact hour-by-hour with a world that most often doesn't understand his way of thinking, his actions and reactions. It's very likely he has already lost the childhood naivete that allows typical children to trust authority figures without much question. Chances are good he has already had more than a few run-ins with adults who, in the words of Jennifer McIlwee Myers, "attempt to use humiliation or public embarrassment to 'teach us a lesson.' We get way too much of that. The only lesson learned is that we can't trust you."

An unconscionable amount of contemporary education is predicated on measurable units of academic knowledge. It's too easy to lose track of the immeasurables, the invaluable building blocks of not only trust, but respect, acceptance, kindness and love. These are not only the foundation under successful learning, but under successful living. The construction of those measurable units of academic knowledge on top of this foundation should not displace it or even take precedence over it.

Jennifer, who gave us an unflinching look at a teacher whose inflexible attitude engendered loathing rather than learning, gives us an opposite but equally startling child's perspective on a teacher who, able to think differently, gained her trust and made an enormous impact in her life:

> One day, the class was in the school library, and we were supposed to be working on our reports. I, however, was just about bouncing off the walls—with all the kids working independently, the library was waaaaaay too chaotic for me to "settle down."
>
> This must have been the umpteenth time that my library behavior had been hyper and inappropriate. My teacher, Mr. Rhine, asked me to step out into the hall with him. Then he did something remarkable.
>
> First, he explained that my behavior was distracting and irritating to the other students, and it would be good if I could not bother them while they were

working. *I did not know this until he told me.* Then he told me that he knew I was very capable of writing the report, but he also knew that I genuinely couldn't settle down and was unable to study in the library with the other students. And then he asked me, what could he do to help me? What did I need to be able to do the work?

I genuinely didn't know. I just knew that whenever we had to all work "independently," I went nuts. I couldn't think of what to tell him.

It didn't matter that I didn't know what to ask for. What mattered to me was that instead of yelling or scolding, he admitted that he didn't understand why I behaved as I did and didn't know how to help me. After years and years of being told I was purposely being a problem, that I was unmotivated and an underachiever, to have a teacher finally admit he just didn't understand what was going on was the most wonderful thing in the world.

He was honest instead of arrogant. Instead of projecting laziness and lack of motivation onto my actions, he admitted his confusion. Since I was confused about my own behavior, too, I could relate and understood his distress.

I never did figure out what to ask him for, but it didn't matter. *I would have crawled through broken glass for that man.* He actually cared and he didn't vilify me for behaviors I couldn't control. I still had lots of problems at school, but I did my best for him.

My "problem" behaviors were and had always been about social cluelessness, sensory issues, and huge amounts of anxiety and fear. Most teachers added to my anxiety, fear and misery by labeling me and stressing me out with their hostile assumptions. Mr. Rhine didn't do that. He was the best teacher I ever had.

I'm with Jennifer. I learned early on that an honest "I don't understand why he does this—but let's try to find out" was a lot more constructive than "He could do it if he really wanted to; he just needs to try harder." The first response arises out of respect and a willingness to learn; the second out of arrogance, a fundamental lack of understanding of autism spectrum disorders—and a fatal lack of curiosity.

Here's an example: I just cringe every time I hear an adult, whether parent or teacher, tell me that this child shouldn't get "special treatment" because it wouldn't be "fair" to the rest of the class or the rest of the family. First of all, accommodation based on neurological need is not "special treatment." Are we extending "special treatment" to the child who must wear glasses to see? Secondly, the concept of "fair" as typical adults understand it is a trap when applied to the child with autism. This explanation of "fair" in my book *Ten Things Every Child with Autism Wishes You Knew* is one for which readers often thank me:

"Fair" is one of those hazy, imprecise terms that is very perplexing to our kid with autism. He doesn't think in terms of fair or unfair, but does know he's having trouble balancing his needs with the rules. As parents, teachers or coaches, we generally think of "fair" as meaning impartial, even-handed, equitable, unbiased. Family rules, school rules, team rules apply to each sibling, student or teammate equally. But autism "un-levels" the playing field. It pot-holes the field. All things are *not* being equal. So our thinking on the subject of "fair" must change. Here it is:

"Fair" does not mean everything is absolutely equal.

"Fair" is when everyone gets what they need.

Really, really look in the mirror on this one. If we are truly honest with ourselves, "no special treatment" is too often a cover-up for, frankly, laziness on our part. At best, it's an unwillingness to acknowledge that we don't know what to do. I recently heard of a mom who refused to divide her batch of cookie dough into two parts, one with nuts and one without, because she "won't cater to" her son with autism. Nuts in cookies suits her, and if he wants a cookie badly enough, he'll eat them with nuts. He has to learn that he can't have things his way—it's her way or no way. No "special treatment" for her son!

That's just ugly and selfish. Any bets on whether her son feels respected, or trusts her to put out any extra effort to do what's best for him? If every moment is a learning moment, what has he learned? Distrust and hypocrisy.

Whether or not one mom can accommodate a legitimate sensory-based no-nuts-in-cookies preference is a microcosm for the whole issue of empowering our student with autism by respecting his differences, developing his ability to make choices and get needs met in a positive manner. Absent those relationship dynamics, trust can't grow. Making good choices is a make-or-break life skill. The child with autism must develop this skill the same as any other child, but for him, he has a distance to travel before even arriving at the starting line. Decision-making skills must be taught, and can only be taught in an atmosphere of trust and empowerment. And like any other skill, competence comes only with practice, and lots of it. Our student with autism might hold out this advice:

Offer me real choices—and only real choices.

- Don't offer me a choice or ask a "Do you want...?" question unless you are willing to accept no for an answer. "No" may be my honest answer to "Do you want to read out loud now?" or "Would you like to share paints with William?" It's hard for me to trust you when the choices you offer are not really choices at all.

  You take for granted the number of choices you have on a daily basis. You constantly choose one option over others knowing that both *having* choices and being *able* to choose provides you control over your life and future. For me, choices are much more limited, which is why it can be harder to feel confident about myself. Provide me with lots of choices so I can practice making decisions and become more involved in my life.

- Whenever possible, change a "have-to" to a choice. Rather than saying: "Write your name and the date on the top of the page," say: "Would you like to write your name first, or would you like to write the date first?" or "Which would you like to write first, letters or numbers?" Follow by showing me: "See how Jason is writing his name on his paper?"

94

- Keep your end of the agreement once I've made a choice. Reducing fifteen minutes of computer time to five because you're running late, or changing the choice mid-stream ("Oh, look, let's do this instead.") erodes my trust in you. Autism means that I think in very concrete, black and white terms: a deal is a deal. That goes both ways.

- Giving me choices helps me learn appropriate behavior, but I also need to understand that there will be times when you can't. When this happens, I won't get as frustrated if I understand why:

  — "I can't give you a choice in this situation because it is dangerous. You might get hurt."

  — "I can't give you that choice because it would be bad for Danny" (have negative effect on another child).

  — "I give you lots of choices but this time it needs to be an adult choice."

This time it needs to be an adult choice. Will we choose to invest the effort in building trust as a precursor to learning and expectation? Will we respect and honor the verbal and behavioral feedback we get from our student with autism as legitimate and valid, and act upon it accordingly? Will we recognize that if we decline to choose, that in fact becomes the choice? Teachers, I can't give you that choice because it would be bad for Danny!

How about this for our new motto:

In trust we trust.

Can I trust you?

Chapter Nine

BELIEVE

Actress Reese Witherspoon looked dazzling in her vintage beaded Dior gown when she accepted her 2005 Academy Award for Best Actress. Her acceptance speech should also achieve vintage status: "I am so blessed to have my...mother and father here. And I just want to say thank you so much for everything, for being so proud of me. It didn't matter if I was making my bed or making a movie. They never hesitated to say how proud they were of me. And that means so very much to a child."

Those who have read any of my work know the thing I most believe in is *believing*—nearly all children, whatever their disability or different ability, have the potential to achieve far beyond what societal stereotypes may suggest. In the previous chapter we talked about trust being the foundation of the teacher-student relationship. The quickest route to building that trust is to nurture and communicate your belief that this child can do it.

> *I can sense far more than I can communicate,* our student with autism tells us, *and the number one thing I can sense is whether or not you think I "can do it." Expecting too little of me is just as bad as expecting too much. Believe that autism imposes no upper limits for me other than the limits of your willingness to stretch as a teacher. Autism is an open-ended disability. There's no telling how far I can go if you lead—not just point—the way.*

That's our job as parents, caregivers, educators, and advocates—to steer the course and keep pushing for the outer limits of our student's potential.

And you may already know what I'm going to say next. Like learning, like behavior, like communication and trust, belief is circular. It goes both ways, all ways. And for better or worse, according to the actions you choose, it is contagious. When you communicate your unfettered belief to your child or student, you encourage him to believe in you as well. That belief in you is what gives him the courage and the impetus to dip his toe into new waters, an incredibly difficult step for many ASD kids. For us, it was a long march requiring relentless patience, but Bryce did finally arrive at a place where he believed in me enough to accept trying new experiences and challenges. He trusted that I would not send him into a situation where he had little chance of success or enjoyment.

Adopting a true belief in your student with autism shouldn't be that hard, given the human race's long-standing willingness to believe in that which they can't actually see just yet. Most major religions are based upon such faith, and literature is filled with such moments. Who among us ever experienced *Peter Pan* without being drawn into the plight of Tinkerbell, who will die unless we believe in her? In Rogers and Hammerstein's memorable *The King and I*, the king soundly berates his children, raised in tropical Siam, for not believing Mrs. Anna's description of snow. She tries to smooth the moment over by reminding him that they've never actually seen snow. "Never seen?" he booms fearsomely. "If they believe only what they see, why do we have school?" Indeed!

My path to achieving True Believer status began with a teacher: Sarah, the adapted PE teacher you met in Chapter Six. Sarah went so many extra miles with Bryce as to constitute a marathon, but her single most striking achievement was to teach him to ride a two-wheel bike. I had struggled for two years (!) trying to teach him. "I will teach him," she said without hesitation. "I will do it on my lunch hour." We brought his bike to school and kept it in a locked equipment closet in the gym. It took her less than forty-five minutes, three fifteen-minute sessions. The long version of how she did it is a story for another book, but the short version unfolded in a conversation we had several years later, when I finally got around to asking Sarah if Bryce's learning experience with the bike was typical for a child with autism.

"Don't know," she said. "Bryce is the first. Actually, only."

"First and only *what*?" I asked, truly puzzled.

"First and only child with autism I ever taught to ride a bike," she replied.

"Get out," I said. "Where are the rest of them?"

"They're not riding bikes."

Back she went into her mantra about belief. Just like Lance Armstrong, it really wasn't about the bike. "You believed that Bryce could do it," she says. "And you instilled that belief in Bryce. Bryce wanted to do it for himself, but he also wanted to do it for you. Not all parents and teachers have that faith in the child, the belief that he or she has the ability to do. The child feels that."

She talked to me for an hour that day, and although she is a PE teacher, very little of what she said was about physical ability or motor skills. "Every kid I've ever worked with," she told me, "has an innate sense of whether the adults in their life believe they can do it." A few half-hour sessions a week with a specialist can only supplement, not compensate for, a belief system at home and in the classroom.

There are many reasons why teachers and parents-as-teachers may lose traction on the road to belief. Sometimes it's simply a matter of being misinformed or uninformed about autism and about the potential in these kids. Current thought is much different than it was even five years ago. But the reason I hear, with startling frequency from professionals who work with our ASD kids, is that parents get stuck in the grief process. While this is certainly true, I think a form of it applies to some teachers too. It may not look or feel like grief and we may not be aware of it at all. But that's exactly what it is if we:

- cap our expectations with thoughts like, "He'll never do that"

- cling to our disappointment over what he will never do instead of celebrating the things at which he's really terrific and encouraging them whole-heartedly

- feel ashamed of or impatient with the behaviors and habits of the child that look odd to the neuro-typical world

- persist in the idea that the child is choosing to be belligerent, lazy or withdrawn—rather than acknowledging that he thinks differently and confronting the difficult work of ferreting out sensory, environmental, social or biochemical triggers.

Grief is always about loss, and it isn't limited to personal relationships; it can apply to professional losses as well. Depression, denial and anger are all part of the grief process, and it's natural that we may either consciously or unconsciously retreat from that which feels like failure. Whether teacher or parent, it's really hard to admit these things about ourselves. But it's the first step to liberating ourselves from them.

This is a critical juncture at which it's so important for team members to support each other. A middle school teacher makes this plea to parents: "Have an honest understanding of the range of your child's disability, but also recognize his strengths. Too often, the most difficult parents to work with are the ones who cannot see the positive qualities of their child. All they can focus on is what the child can't do. Perhaps they do not want to have a child with a disability; perhaps they are stuck in the grieving process. See the positive in your child."

Sarah's formula for success is simple, and it works with any kind of learning. It is this:

Repetition breeds familiarity.

Familiarity breeds confidence.

Confidence brings belief.

Belief brings action.

Ability, disability, or different ability-it is truly only part of the picture. The seeds of a child's success rest in you.

Here are the six most important things you can do for your student with autism. I call them The Rules of Believing:

1. Believe she can do it. Really believe.

2. Then go beyond merely believing—to act on the belief is what makes it happen for your student. Actively seek out and place him in situations where he will experience success. Look for opportunities where she can lead, such as organizing the art show or reading a favorite book to the kindergarten class. Remember Jennifer's story about the teacher who refused to capitalize on her interest in dictionaries? That was an opportunity lost, taken to a shameful degree.

3. If you are a parent, remember that you are a teacher, too. Involve yourself. "Don't fall into a pass-your-kid-off mentality, whether it's six hours a day in school, or forty-five minutes three times a week in an after-school activity," Sarah says. Play with her, take her places, read with and to her. Watch how she does things; try to see how she learns and where she needs help. Work out how you can break down challenging tasks into smaller pieces for her. *Be curious* about her.

4. Involve family, friends, people at school-everyone in his world. The more reinforcement a child has, the more he'll progress and the more he will let others in. Bryce was surprised, then delighted, when his teachers attended his swim meets and his community theatre performances. Two of his friends joined his baseball team after hearing about it from us.

5. Siblings play a very important role in this. Siblings have much to learn from each other. Allow and encourage them to play together and participate together in whatever manner seems appropriate to their current age and stage of childhood. My sons will always have fond memories of their years together on swim team. Bryce was proud of Connor being the team's captain, and Connor was even more proud of Bryce earning the team's Most Improved Award.

6. Allow your student or child to be who she is— which may not be what you expect. It bears repeating: Where the expectation is too high, it can turn the child off completely to the very things you desire for her. Where the expectation is too low, gifts and talents go undiscovered.

7. Throw out any growth or developmental milestone lists or charts you get from pediatricians, books, or websites. They are irrelevant to your student with autism. Every child, regardless of ability or disability, is going to grow and develop at his own pace. "It's not about doing it in any specific order or in any specific way." Sarah says. "Children will flourish if they are nurtured and if their way of doing things is celebrated."

As teachers and parent-teachers, what we want for our student with autism can probably be described with a common vocabulary. Positive results. Forward movement as well as lateral growth. What we have to ask ourselves is this: in deed and in thought, is what we are doing now moving toward or away from those goals? What do we believe of this child, and will that belief bring us forward movement, or not? All motion is relative—we need only stand still, and those goals will move farther and farther away.

Somewhere in my long-ago adventures as an elementary school student, a teacher gave me a copy of Walter Wintle's poem "The Man Who Thinks He Can," which begins:

> If you think you're beaten, you are.
> If you think you dare not, you don't.
> If you'd like to win, but you think you can't,
> It's almost a cinch you won't.

That poem never really left me, but it started bubbling to the surface of my consciousness more frequently once I had children, and especially once I realized that my children would face a steeper uphill climb in life than most. I started to realize that *if* was a powerful qualifier. But the choice was mine whether it would be one of constraint—as in ifs, ands and buts—or one of possibility, as in Wintle's poem.

You don't have to call it belief. You can call it "positive thinking." Or you can call it "self-fulfilling prophecy." You can call it anything you want. But in today's over-hyped, ultra-competitive, measured-to-a-gnat's-eye, give-everything-a-score society, I had to give my special kids something more real, more lasting, something that would give them roots during our time together, and at the same time give them wings when the time came for them to venture forth on their own—whether for an hour, a week or a lifetime. As my teacher had done thirty-five years earlier, I gave them Wintle's poem:

> Life's battles don't always go to the stronger or faster man.
>
> Sooner or later the one who wins is the one who THINKS he can.

Chapter Ten

TEACH ME "HOW TO FISH"
See me as a capable adult and hold that vision.

One of the luckiest breaks I ever caught was the school district geography that landed us with Teacher Christine as Bryce's first special educator. Even before my head stopped spinning from the initial identification of autism, even before I began to learn what autism was, she told me clearly all the things that autism wasn't: it wasn't shameful, it wasn't a death sentence, or even a life-without-parole sentence and it wasn't a stereotype ("They are not all headbangers.") It hurts terribly to hear the word *autism* or *autistic* applied to your child, she said, I understand. But the label is the means to the services. You want the services, because...

He is a Potentially Independent Adult.

With those three little words, I knew instantly what my long-range goal was: to leave this planet knowing that Bryce would be okay without me. I'd have to teach him to fish. As a child with autism, teaching him to fish would require far more of me than merely leading him to the river and throwing the line in the water. He had to walk before he ran; he would need to become an independent student and child before he could become an independent adult.

The road to independent adulthood starts with this: that your student or child be able to handle independently as much of his "day job"—being a student—as possible. Right from the beginning, instill independent-living habits and skills—let him do as much for himself as possible, with *patient instruction* from you.

That directive is worth dissecting. *Patient*: because your student with autism may require many, many repetitions of a skill before becoming competent at it. And he has two strikes against him because, unlike his typically-developing peers, he may have far fewer opportunities to practice those skills. It is our responsibility as teachers and as parent-teachers to create the additional opportunities he needs, and moreover to maintain patience through the process, however long it may be. *Instruction*: not intervention or doing it for him in the name of helping, because the goal is that he do it himself. And implicit in the responsibility to instruct is that we do it in a manner that is appropriate to his learning style.

The importance of promoting independence can hardly be overstated. Many teachers are parents themselves; they understand the time-stress continuum most families function within. But whether it's homework or personal organization, expedience in the moment will impede your student with autism from learning to be independent in the long run. If you pack and unpack his backpack for him every day, how will he learn the importance of being organized, knowing where things are when they are needed, how to find items or information? The same applies to putting together his lunch, completing the last two math problems or zipping his own jacket. I'm a mother and I do understand, sometimes in the morning or evening time crunch, it just seems quicker to do it for him. But learning to organize his work and his time, being able to manage his own clothes and money, learning to use all manner of implements are the skills that will bring him autonomy, and he will only learn them through patient repetition.

Teach me RELEVANCE

Teach me relevance, our student with autism would say. Math problems in a workbook don't seem to have a purpose. How is this skill useful to me? Teach me whether or not I have enough money for groceries today, and what's the difference between a teaspoon and a tablespoon if I want to make a cake? Spelling isn't about a list of words on a page, or being able to spell "exponential" without knowing what it means. It's learning to spell so that I can fill out a job application and write a complaint letter when the landlord won't fix the leak in the roof. More than being able to find Estonia on a map of the world, I need to be able to find the library on a map of my city.

Even in our outstanding school, there were moments when I nearly wept with frustration at the utter irrelevance of how the curriculum was being applied to my son with autism. In late elementary school, Bryce was given beginner level instruction in how to do Internet research. Of course this is a valuable, necessary skill in contemporary education and life. I was very excited to hear about it until I saw the practice worksheet. He had been assigned to look up things like who won the Grammy for Best Female Singer the year he was born, and what year Spain and Portugal had signed the Treaty of Tordesillas. Neither of these pieces of information had any relevance whatsoever to him. You can imagine the effect on his interest in learning this skill: flatter than day-old root beer. Without the ability to generalize the skill (Chapter Three in action), it was another good year or so before he was fully able to comprehend that the Internet was a great source for information that both interested and helped him. The point of the original lesson had been to introduce a computer skill. How little effort it would have taken to modify that original assignment to have him look up something either functional or relevant to him—such as which local parks have bike paths, or what the weather was going to be that weekend. A pasta recipe or how the Hershey company got started or a biography of J. K. Rowling. *Functional!* was (and is) my mantra at IEP meetings. I want him *functional!* Which, not coincidentally, includes the word *fun.*

And fun is indeed the beginnings of functional. All children learn more eagerly through fun, and your student with autism is no exception. Fun is the doorway to exploration, exploration is the doorway to motivation and motivation is key to learning. The common ingredient to both fun and motivation is relevance. On the road to independence, your student will learn any skill much more quickly if, and possibly only if, you make it relevant to his life and interests. Think of yourself in your own work, and how deeply you resent "busywork." With finite energy and time, all of us want our efforts to be applicable to our goals. Your student with autism is no different.

We have now spent a whole book discussing how children with autism think differently, process differently and experience our world differently. But in coming to a clearer understanding of them, we remind ourselves again that this whole child is a child who will develop normally in many ways, who will still have many things in common with typically-developing kids. The need for independent living skills is universal among all of us who want to live self-sufficiently as adults, and the fact that a child has autism doesn't release us from our obligation to teach those skills, it only dictates that they be taught in a manner understandable to an autism way of thinking.

We identify and remove the sensory and environmental barriers to learning, we teach in language that is appropriate and comprehensible to them, we break large tasks into smaller pieces. We teach them to be functional within their autism—not to replicate "typical" children. Jennifer McIlwee Myers advises, "Please don't try to make us 'normal.' We'd much rather be functional. It's hard to be functional when you have to spend all your time and energy focusing on not tapping your feet." To be comfortable and happy with themselves is as much the birthright of the child with autism as it is any other child's.

We teach the indispensable intangibles, like being a friend in order to have a friend, accepting that no one is perfect, that "mistake" is just another word for "let's try again." We guide them to understanding that no one is a mind-reader, and that asking questions is not only a means of getting information, but a means to connecting with people as well.

We teach the intangibles knowing that the "eureka" moment may not in fact be a moment but more like a sunrise—a slow but rosy dawning of awareness. We trust in the (possibly imperceptible) process of progression that will get us there.

Then we let go. In carefully planned and staged increments, one-step-at-a-time "confidence bricks" on that road to adulthood.

Teach me SELF-RELIANCE

Teach me what self-reliance is and the googolplex of possibilities it brings me, our student with autism might say. *Show me how becoming a do-it-myself person—learning to fish—builds the confidence to know that I can succeed in new situations, be among all kinds of people, understand that challenges can be hard work, but also worthwhile and fun. Deep inside, I really want this, even if I appear fearful of it at the outset. If I don't learn to be self-reliant, I will always be dependent on you or someone else. In the end, that drags both of us down.*

Many educators are familiar with the term "scaffolding" as it relates to teaching. Metaphorically, it is not different from its concrete definition in the construction industry. Scaffolding is the temporary structure that supports workers while a permanent building is under construction. When the permanent structure is complete and support no longer needed, the scaffolding is removed. Scaffolding can range from simple to elaborate, and its removal may happen in stages. But the end result is the same—a stand-alone structure.

Scaffolding as an educational strategy is the same, and is particularly useful for developing self-sufficiency in a student with autism. We teach and model, we up the challenges one "floor" at a time, we remove the supports as each new level of self-reliance is achieved. Removing the support—letting go—is a process, not an event, for both the student and the teacher.

An essential part of the journey toward self-sufficiency is learning to deal with adversity. Accepting our inherent fallibility as human beings is a tall order for many people. But for the student with autism, it is an even more towering challenge because mistakes may only come in two sizes: non-existent or crushing. Use scaffolding not just in teaching and building, but in allowing for incremental failure. Set the stage for little mistakes that lead to his ability to handle increasingly larger "misfortunes."

I recall a psychologist who spent an afternoon observing a group of toddlers playing at the park. He noted that the mothers fell into two groups: the "kaboom!" mommies and the "oh no!" mommies. When the fast-moving toddlers would inevitably get ahead of their feet and go splat in the grass or the sawdust, the "kaboom!" mommies would say "kaboom!" with smiles and clapping and an "up you go, now!" And the "kaboom!" kids would do just that. The "oh no!" mommies, on the other hand, would leap up with cries of "are you okay?" and rush to brush off a toddler who often took mom's reaction as a cue to burst into tears.

Attitude is everything. Your attitude towards your student or child is going to be that child's attitude towards himself. If you can't see him and celebrate him as a capable, interesting, productive and valuable member of the classroom, the family and the community, no amount of "education" or "therapy" you layer on top is going to matter.

Teach a man to fish and you feed him for a lifetime.

By teaching our student with autism to fish, we arrive back where we started at the beginning of this book: proof positive that learning is circular. Because the ten things your student with autism wants you to know are the very ten things that he also needs to know and live in order to fulfill that vision of a capable independent adult. He embraces his role as a life-long learner and teacher, he is connected to others as part of a team—actually, part of many different teams as family member, co-worker, neighbor, citizen. He understands and accepts responsibility for his own behavior, and he effectively communicates needs, wants and information. He understands his own unusual way of thinking and how he must adapt to a world that thinks differently than he does.

He sees himself a whole, brilliantly-faceted person, and he likes what he sees. He believes in himself. *He* has the vision of a capable, independent adult.

He is curious about his world. *I wonder* how far he can go now?

Like Dorothy opening the door to Oz, his world has changed from black-and-white to technicolor. Like Bryce on that last day at Capitol Hill School, he is off and running, shirttails flying. Run, Bryce, run on! His teachers, those incomparable teammates, can only wave from the sidewalk. In his hand is the Great Tackle Box of Life, and we feel sure that on a wonderful day yet to come, we will see what we always believed—that he has truly

Endnotes

Chapter Three
I Think Differently
Veronica Zysk, co-author

Unwritten Rules of Social Relationships, © 2005 Dr. Temple Grandin and Sean Barron.

Thinking of YOU Thinking of ME: Philosophies and strategies to further develop perspective taking and communicative abilities for persons with Social Cognitive Deficits, © 2002 Michelle Garcia Winner.

Chapter Four
Behavior is Communication: Yours, Mine and Ours

"Behavior can cause unwanted results." *Some Extremely Reasonable Suggestions for 'Typical' Parents, Family, and Teachers on Behalf of Kids With Asperger's Syndrome,* © 2004 Jennifer McIlwee Myers.

Chapter Five
Glitched Garbled and Bewildered

"Idioms and Metaphors and Things that Go Bump in Their Heads." Postcards from the Road Less Traveled, *Autism Asperger's Digest,* January-February 2005, © 2005 Ellen Notbohm.

Ten Things Every Child with Autism Wishes You Knew. ©2005 Ellen Notbohm, Chapter Four, "I am a Concrete Thinker."

Ten Things Every Child with Autism Wishes You Knew. ©2005 Ellen Notbohm, Chapter Eight, "Please Help Me with Social Interactions."

Chapter Six
Teach the Whole Me

"Ready for K...and Beyond." Postcards from the Road Less Traveled, *Autism-Asperger's Digest*, March-April 2006 © 2006 Ellen Notbohm

"Dress Rehearsal." *1001 Great Ideas for Teaching and Raising Children with Autism Spectrum Disorders*, © 2004 Ellen Notbohm and Veronica Zysk, Chapter 4, "To Do and Understand."

"When Math Doesn't Add Up." Postcards from the Road Less Traveled, Autism Asperger's Digest, January-February 2006, © 2006 Ellen Notbohm.

Chapter Seven
Be Curious...be very curious

Ten Things Every Child with Autism Wishes You Knew, ©2005 Ellen Notbohm, Chapter Nine, "Try to Figure Out What Triggers My Meltdowns."

Chapter Eight
Can I Trust You?

"Choice is Good." *1001 Great Ideas for Teaching and Raising Children with Autism Spectrum Disorders*, © 2004 Ellen Notbohm and Veronica Zysk, Chapter 6, "Learners and Doers."

"...attempt to use public embarrassment to 'teach us a lesson.'"*Some Extremely Reasonable Suggestions for 'Typical' Parents, Family, and Teachers on Behalf of Kids With Asperger's Syndrome* © 2004 Jennifer McIlwee Myers.

Chapter 9
Believe

*"The Difference Between Heaven and Earth."*Postcards from the Road Less Traveled, *Autism-Asperger's Digest*, May-June 2005, © 2005 Ellen Notbohm.

"The Rules of Believing." Exceptional Children: Navigating Special Education, *Children's Voice*, January -February 2006, © 2006 Ellen Notbohm.

Chapter 10
Teach Me "How to Fish"

"Please don't try to make us 'normal.'" *Some Extremely Reasonable Suggestions for 'Typical' Parents, Family, and Teachers on Behalf of Kids With Asperger's Syndrome,* © 2004 Jennifer McIlwee Myers

Ellen's articles can be requested through her website at www.ellennotbohm.com

About the Author

Book author, columnist and mother of sons with autism and ADHD, Ellen Notbohm's writings on autism and general interest subjects have been published on every continent (except Antarctica—yet). Her previous book, *Ten Things Every Child with Autism Wishes You Knew* was a ForeWord 2005 Book of the Year Honorable Mention winner and recipient of a 2005 iParenting Media Award. A regular columnist for *Autism-Asperger's Digest* magazine and *Children's Voice*, she also co-authored with Veronica Zysk *1001 Great Ideas for Teaching and Raising Children with Autism Spectrum Disorders*, a *Learning Magazine* 2006 Teachers' Choice Award winner.

Ellen welcomes reader feedback through her website at www.ellennotbohm.com.